Ridg

MW00939670

~

A memoir of Appalachia

~~~~~~~

By Chris Wohlwend

Copyright © 2019

PRESS

Sections of this book appeared on the websites LikeTheDew.com and Ridgerunning.com. Others were published in The Knoxville Mercury. The JR Buchanan profile originally appeared in The Atlanta Journal-Constitution. All are reprinted here with permission.

This memoir of growing up in Knoxville could not have happened without the help of many of those who experienced it with me. Some are identified in the stories with which they are associated; the names of others have been changed.

Keystroke Press
216 Sarvis Drive
Knoxville, TN 37920

Table of Contents

Introduction

Growing Up
Grandchild of the Depression – Escape from Rose Hill – Alligators and "panters" – Chicken thieves and a drowning – Lessons learned in the Boy Scouts – Exploding toilets and zip guns at Park Junior High – Four-barrel Baptists

License to Roam
Tales of the Midway – Playing Santa Claus – Food fights and creative cussing – Rampage on the bread route – A late-night trip to jail – Killian's '51 Ford

Working
Blue notes, bandstands, and roadhouses – Faces of tragedy – Bank robbers and burgers – Tondalaya and the long-legged June Knight – Stakeouts and close calls in the private-dick trade

A Sixties Education
Doc and the Cowboy – Sweet William – Poolrooms and the Knoxville Bear – Squeegee and other Strip characters – Moonshine in the mountains – Up the creek with Jim Dykes – Playmate of the Year – Lenny and the hooker – Going to the game with Rod

Character Studies

Ben Byrd and other Sports – Fires in the pressroom – Racial realities in the boxing ring – Ace and Big John Tate – River rats and snaked dates – Coeds, and an armed neighbor on Clinch Avenue – Beer and peanuts on Christmas eve

Leaving Campus

Sleeping in bear country – A mountain man and marijuana – The Wall of Death – President Nixon at Neyland Stadium – Carp Surprise and other antics in Society – Fire in the newsroom – The two-gun bookie – Mystery at Brother Jack's

Preparing for Departure

A Sixties' soundtrack – Streaking and tragedy on the Strip – Streetcar, Speedy and other drunks – Sexcapades with the Duffer – The script girl and a missed opportunity – "Banty roosters" and cockfights – Union organizing – Setting the stage for the next chapter

Introduction

One Sunday night in the mid-1960s, when I was working at a low-level editing job at Knoxville's morning newspaper, the police reporter got a story tip.

The cops were working to rescue a jumper off the Gay Street Bridge, a couple of blocks from the newspaper office. The bridge spanned the Tennessee River between the courthouse on the downtown side and a hospital complex on the other. It was a popular starting point for those seeking permanent escape from their troubles.

The reporter and a photographer hurried down to the bridge. There, they beheld an absurd sight. The jumper had miscalculated – he was too close to the hospital side of the river and had landed in the mud flats alongside the river. The spotlights from the rescue squad on the bridge showed him up to his armpits in the mud, arms spread as he looked forlornly up at his would-be rescuers.

His plight had come to the attention of the police after a call from one of the student nurses in the hospital's dorm. She and her roommates had heard faint yells for help.

Sundays are generally slow news days, which meant that the hapless jumper made the front page of the Monday paper. He turned out to be a drunk known to the police, an Appalachia native who had drifted to Knoxville seeking work. He was, as

I realized years later, just another East Tennessean trying to get away from his fate, choosing the ultimate escape in his alcohol-fogged condition.

Knoxville – where I was born and grew up – is nestled in the valley of the Tennessee River between the Great Smoky Mountains on the east and the Cumberland Plateau on the west. Situated on a navigable waterway, it was in its early days a departure spot for what has come to be called the Old West. As such, its early history was rough and tumble, attributes that in many ways still define it.

The would-be suicide was, unfortunately, typical of his southern-Appalachian brethren. He was, another native explained to me decades later, "only guilty of being drunk and poor."

In college at the University of Tennessee, I learned that the area's terrain is called "ridge and valley." I already knew about the terrain, having grown up in a house that was, typical for the area, "dug" into the side of a ridge, but I had not been aware of the official terminology.

When my friends and I first obtained driver licenses in the late 1950s, we took to exploring the ridges and valleys in the family vehicles. We called it ridge running, and we roamed up and down the valleys that run northeast to southwest, sometimes in daylight but more often in the dark of night – most of us only had access to vehicles when our dads got home from work.

Our wandering often led to encounters with rural natives, in hamlets like Wears Valley and Rutledge, in Washburn and

Crab Orchard, in Spillcorn and up on Hogskin Creek. These encounters broadened our knowledge: We gained first-hand experience with moonshine and with girls who were looking to escape the farms where they grew up. But mostly our ridge running was about our own escape – we simply were looking for something to do. By the time I graduated high school and enrolled at the University of Tennessee, I was a veteran ridge-runner.

I was born as 1945 was drawing to a close, when the world was still teetering from World War II and from the Great Depression. But my first memories are from about 1949, when there was an aura of optimism. It wasn't until decades later that I started to get an understanding of what underlay the culture in which I grew up.

My real education began after I snagged a job as a copy boy (a clerk) at The Knoxville Journal when I was a sophomore at UT. I soon realized that the mountains and valleys were home to hard-working and hard-living folks. Many of them had not ventured far from the isolated ridges and valleys where they were reared. And some of them were leery – if not outright resentful – of city dwellers. But many others sought escape, travelling first to Knoxville and then on to the larger world.

I had learned a bit about my dad's upbringing by listening as he and his friends sat around talking and laughing about their escapades growing up in the east-Knoxville section known as Burlington. But it wasn't until my father's death in 1993 that my mother opened up about the Depression and its effect on her childhood. She also provided details about the background of my taciturn dad, who had not shared his childhood memories with us.

My ancestors were typical of East Tennessee and of Appalachia: Scots-Irish on my mother's side, Swiss-German on my father's.

I didn't find out until decades after her death, but my dad's mom was descended from English adventurers who landed at Jamestown on the Atlantic coast of what became Virginia in the early 17th century. Restless and ambitious, within a couple of generations they had moved far enough west to carve toeholds on the eastern edge of the mountains in the valleys that became stopping points on Daniel Boone's Wilderness Road. Mrs. Wohlwend came by a bent for adventure quite naturally. And, through her, so did I.

My father's adventurous nature did not involve traveling so much, but he was not afraid of taking a chance. When still a teen-ager, he left his crowded home (there were seven younger siblings), moving first into his German-speaking grandmother's house just down the road, then into an apartment. He dropped out of high school and was soon working at a service station in Burlington, hanging out with like-minded neighborhood buddies. The stories I heard years later as they reminisced involved unguarded boxcars and bootleggers and bank robbers.

By the time I was driving age, I was a veteran of bicycle rides all over Burlington, where we were living. My friends Jimmy Britton and Danny Meador and I would sometimes stay out well after dark, roaming the night streets.

There were narrow escapes, to be sure: Hiding from the occasional patrolling police car (we were never caught, so I guess we became adept at it); being chased away by the angry parents of girls we were trying to coax out to join us. Once, when the father of one of our female friends came out suddenly and we couldn't get to our bikes, we scrambled under a parked car and nervously watched his shoes as he walked around looking for us.

One night we noticed smoke coming from the Hollow, a woods of several acres just over the hill from my house. There, we found two acquaintances from the "wrong" side of the ridge. Foxx and Crowder, as I'll call them here, had a fire going and were roasting a chicken, scattered feathers attesting to its freshness. It had, they proudly told us, belonged to a neighbor a half hour earlier.

They invited us to join them the next night, and we told them "sure," knowing that we had no intention of becoming chicken thieves before we even had our driver's licenses.

By the time we made it to high school, our heroes included Moocher Cain and Tommy Mitchell – they not only had their own Chevies, but they had customized them. Moocher had a cherry '56, Tommy a '37 painted an attention-grabbing metallic purple.

When we finally got our own driver's licenses, we suddenly had real freedom. Sure, we depended on our parents' good graces for vehicles, but now we could drive to Burlington's drive-in restaurants – the Tic Toc, the Pizza Palace, the Blue Circle – or farther afield to Cherokee Lake or to the Whittle Springs Swimming Pool.

As we progressed in our abilities to cajole the family station wagons (and gas money) and as our curfews were extended, we made trips of 40 or 50 miles. We would check the local teen hangouts, cruise the A&W in Madisonville or Carl's Drive-in outside of Loudon, investigate a rumored haunted house in Sevier County, go sledding at Newfound Gap in the Great Smoky Mountains National Park.

My first real job, when I was a college freshman, involved a vehicle. I made deliveries for Swan's Sunbeam Bakery on Sundays, driving a bread truck.

But it was my second job, at the Journal, where I honed my knowledge of ridge running, discovering some of the more remote hollows with some of my co-workers. Because we didn't get off work until 2 a.m., we became familiar with the denizens of the darker hours, knew where the all-night hangouts were, both those that were legit and those that were not.

And I discovered that many of my fellow Appalachia dwellers nursed the same wanderlust, the same curiosity about the unusual.

Many of the ones who made the pages of the newspaper fell into the wrong-side-of-the-ridge category of Foxx and Crowder, and their bent for adventure frequently led them into trouble. The Sunday-night jumper was only one example.

One of the more extraordinary was a doctor from upper East Tennessee who was found bleeding in a room at the Monday Hotel across from the Trailways Bus Station on a weekend night. He had made the trip to Knoxville to pick up one of the young men he favored. After whiskey fortification, he had talked his new friend into castrating him, providing the necessary tools and instructions. The youth panicked at the first sight of blood and ran from the room, then made an anonymous call to the police. Despite losing some blood, the doctor wasn't seriously hurt and was soon on his way home.

Most of the stories that made the Journal, of course, ended more tragically. And it wasn't until I had moved on – to Europe and then other newspaper jobs, in Miami, Charlotte, Louisville, Dallas, Kansas City and Atlanta, that I realized that many of the characters I had encountered in my Journal duties were, perhaps, a bit out of step with those who are generally classified as "civilized people."

Like the would-be suicide and the doctor, they all possessed a certain hard-headed – wrong-headed in many cases – determination. Many made their marks outside of the law, but others stuck in my memory because of their resolve to escape the hollows and the ridges. Here, then are the stories – reconstructed as best I can remember them, most of the names changed – of some of those Appalachians. Several I was related to; others I encountered while at the university during the tumultuous years of the Sixties, some were featured in accounts told in The Knoxville Journal, and still others were the subjects of stories I wrote years later. The one thing they had in common? They were all ridge runners.

Growing up

Grandchild of the Depression – Escape from Rose Hill – Alligators and "panters" – Chicken thieves and tragedy – Lessons learned in the Boy Scouts – Exploding toilets and zip guns at Park Junior High – Four-barrel Baptists

~~~~~~~~~~~

IN THE PHOTOGRAPH, my mother, Opal Christine Monday, is in her late teens. On a bicycle, she is flanked by two young men dressed in suit and tie. One is smiling at the camera, the other is writing something.

When I first saw the image shortly after my dad died in 1993, I wondered who the men were and what was going on. My mother had four brothers, but the men in the picture did not appear to be any kin that I knew.

After Dad's death at age 79, Mom, perhaps beginning to come to terms with her own mortality, had been opening up about being a child of the Great Depression. Neither she nor my dad had ever discussed the hard times in the presence of my siblings and me. So I showed her the picture and asked what was going on.

"Oh," she said, "That's those two deaf and dumb boys" using the terminology of her generation, with an inflection assuming that I knew whom she was talking about.

What two "deaf and dumb boys," I wanted to know.

"The ones I rented a room to," she replied. "He's writing a check for the rent."

My mother collecting rent in Burlington
from a pair of boarders at her house, circa 1940.

And that was the beginning of the story I got from her, a story that was both remarkable and explanatory, exposing a background that revealed much about her personality.

When I was growing up in Burlington, we lived only a few blocks from my mother's parents, B.L. and Etta Monday. Their house on Lakeside Street was a basic two-bedroom, one bath, typical of the time it was built, the early 1920s. But my grandfather, a skilled carpenter, had replaced the original outhouse with a spacious bathroom. Plus, he had built a large garage/workshop alongside the back alley. The workshop, where he spent much of his time, had its own coal-burning stove.

That house, my mother was now telling me, had been purchased after they had to give up a larger, two-story dwelling on Fern Street several blocks away, because my grandfather had lost his job selling life insurance after the stock-market crash of 1929.

The fall came after he had built up his business enough so that he was dividing his time between Knoxville and Nashville, riding the train between the two cities. He had diversified by opening a grocery with his brother in Beaumont, the north-Knoxville neighborhood where he and my grandmother grew up. His brother ran the store. They lost the grocery shortly before foreclosure on the Fern Street house.

Papaw Monday struggled to find work, finally landing a blue-collar position at Cherokee Mills, one of Knoxville's many textile operations. He supplemented that income with carpentry jobs.

How did he afford to buy the house they lived in when I came along?

My mother, then still in her teens, provided the $200 down payment. She had been working various jobs while in high school, saving everything she could.

She had clerked in a dry-goods store in Burlington. That was followed by a stint selling men's shirts door-to-door. "One of the salesmen we bought from offered me the job," she explained.

Then, with the advent of World War II, she said, "Me and Martha Miles moved to Fort Worth for jobs in an airplane plant." Martha was one of her close friends.

She returned to Knoxville for a position as a crane operator at the Aluminum Company of America's giant facility in adjoining Blount County. There, she was re-acquainted with Vernon Wohlwend, an Alcoa machinist who had also grown up in Burlington. Soon, they were married.

Wohlwend Brothers Farm, on rich bottomland along the Holston River just east of Burlington, was created and maintained by his dad and two uncles. The Depression had not affected them as much as it had the Mondays – demand for food didn't evaporate like demand for life insurance.

The different backgrounds led to a lifelong conflict. My dad wasn't particularly ambitious money-wise, content with what he earned at Alcoa thanks to the strides made by the

United Steelworkers, the union that represented the company's workers.

My mother, still fueled by the same ambition that led her door-to-door with men's shirts, pushed Dad to be more aggressive about being promoted, to move into management. Once, when I was about 12 years old, I overheard an argument that piqued my interest. Dad had been offered a position at an Alcoa facility in Trinidad and Mom wanted him to take it. He didn't want to leave Burlington and all his friends, certainly not for a small island in the Caribbean. He prevailed.

I was disappointed. As so often happens, a family trait had skipped a generation: I already had his mother's wanderlust. Mamaw Wohlwend had, according to her husband, "been born with one foot in the road."

Like most women of her generation, she had never learned to drive. So she would badger other family members for "a run up to Rogersville" or "down to Madisonville" to visit cousins. The former is north of Knoxville, the latter south, hence the "up" and "down" usage. Both are far enough away so that such a trip was a day-long endeavor at that pre-interstate time.

There was passenger-train service to Madisonville, but there was no depot. Dad occasionally made the trip when he was young. "I had to tell the conductor I wanted off," he told me, "and the train would stop. To catch it coming back I'd have to stand near the tracks and flag the train."

Such behavior was not suited to his prim and proper mother, though she made use of local public transportation. My earliest memory of Mamaw Wohlwend is of her walking toward our house in Burlington after getting off the bus a block away. By then Papaw Wohlwend was retired and they were living in south Knox County, about 20 miles from our house. She could catch a White Star Lines bus on its way to Knoxville from Maryville, then transfer to the local McCalla Avenue bus to get to our house. But she suffered a stroke shortly after my mental picture of her walking down the street. She was left bedridden, though her mental capacity was not affected.

The Wohlwends, in serious mode, circa 1920. My dad, the first-born child, stands at his mother's left shoulder.

We visited once a week, Mom and Dad in the parlor where she was, my siblings and I playing outside with whichever cousins were present. We searched for crawdads in a nearby creek, or, during spring and summer, raided Papaw's garden for strawberries, peanuts, and melons. So my childhood memories of grandparents are divided between east Knoxville and rural south Knox County.

~~~~~~~~~~

MOM'S DEAF-MUTE renters were not the only boarders to use the room that was emptied once Mom's brothers had moved out, three into the army during World War II, the other to a defense-industry job in southern California.

The first boarder that I remember was trying to escape a hard-scrabble life a hundred miles north. I was about 3 years old when Norma showed up at the front door on Lakeside.

In her late teens, she had left her home in rural southwestern Virginia, catching the bus to Knoxville in hopes of finding a job.

The trip was Norma's first to Knoxville, and she exited the bus when it reached Burlington, mistakenly believing the business bustle she was seeing meant that she had reached the city. The highway, U.S. 11/70, became Magnolia Avenue at Burlington, morphing into a prosperous-looking four-lane. She was unaware that she was still several miles from downtown. Noticing a help-wanted sign in the window of Kay's ice-cream parlor at Magnolia and Crawford Street, she walked in and applied. She was immediately hired as counter help.

Next, she needed a place to live, and my grandparents' house was only a block or so from Kay's. Mamaw Monday let Norma stay in the spare bedroom, and she helped around the house for her board. Soon, she was helping my mother, who was trying to manage me, a handful like most toddlers, and my new baby sister. Norma began spending a lot of time at our place, within walking distance of my grandparents' house.

Norma soon added another job, working the night shift at Standard Knitting Mills – she could get there on the city bus that stopped in front of Kay's, exiting at Winona Street and walking the last few blocks.

I was too young to understand all this, and my memories of Norma from that time aren't clear. But I knew that she was important to our household and to my grandmother's as well.

But Norma's ambition went beyond the mill and the ice-cream counter. She saved her money until she had enough to enroll in beauty school. By the time I was a student at Park Junior High School in Park City, she had married and was the proprietor of her own beauty salon in Burlington. Soon, she was rearing her own family.

Years later, my mother and dad provided details about Norma, whose tale was typical of the time and place, a story of want, ambition and determination.

Norma Jean Lee had grown up in Rose Hill, Virginia, and did not see a future in what was around her. Belying its name, Rose Hill is a mean stop in coal-mining country, another ridge-side Appalachian hamlet where residents eke out a living as best they can. There were several brothers and sisters. And, according to my parents, the family did not want Norma Jean heading south to the metropolis of Knoxville.

A couple of months after her arrival in Burlington, my dad said, Norma was confronted by her mother, who had ridden the bus to Knoxville to take her daughter back home. Norma refused, and there were shouts and then tears. When her mother left, Dad remembered, Norma looked at him and said, "I don't care if they do come after me, I'm never going back to Rose Hill."

Next, a younger sister came down to see if she could persuade Norma to return. She succumbed to Knoxville's city charms.

"Norma took her on the bus downtown to the movie at the Tennessee Theater," my mother said. "They got caught in the rain, and got soaked. Norma's sister only had the dress she was wearing, so she had to stay another day until her dress dried out." She caught the bus back to Rose Hill the next day, returning without her sister.

True to her vow, Norma only returned when she died in 1991, aged 62, to be buried in Rose Hill's Daniels Cemetery.

~~~~~~~~~~

LAKESIDE STREET got its name because it formed the eastern boundary of Chilhowee Park, home of Lake Ottosee. And, according to my mother, the lake provided recreation and fishing for her brothers. Two of them, Kenneth and Maynard, she told me once, were responsible for the founding of the Knoxville Zoo. They were assisted by two baby alligators that were briefly domiciled in the lake.

Of course, the park had its own native wildlife – songbirds and squirrels and rabbits, with lots of ducks and fish in the lake. So my uncles can be forgiven for thinking that alligators would be a natural, if not altogether welcome, addition.

One summer in the late 1930s, as my mother told the story, Kenneth and Maynard, then in their late teens, made a trip to Florida. There, they discovered tourist stops that sold live baby alligators. And they decided that *alligator mississipiensis* would be right at home in Burlington.

Their motives, as my mother related them, were completely innocent. She contended that they did not think of introducing them into Lake Ottosee, that they believed that my grandmother would welcome them into the household. Besides, she said, they were not thinking about the gators multiplying – they thought both babies were male, even naming them Kenneth and Maynard. Or maybe it was my grandmother who bestowed the monikers. My mother said she could not remember for sure.

But conversations that I had with my uncles when I was a teen-ager made me think that their intent was more devious, that, from the beginning, they saw the lake as the natural home for the pair.

Understandably, my grandmother wasn't enamored of the horny new arrivals. A dog and a cat were pets enough, she reasoned. (The chickens that had the run of the backyard were not pets – they were there to supply food.) So, before they had time to make friends with the dog and cat, before they had grown enough to take more than a passing interest in the chickens, the gators were transported to the lake and set free.

Initially, it being summer and the water being studded with fuzzy ducklings, Kenneth and Maynard had easy pickings at mealtime. But as the ducklings and the gators matured mealtime became noisier, with whipping tails and panicky squawking and feathery splashing. Children fishing from the banks for sunfish took notice. Soon, Kenneth and Maynard were well on their way to becoming the stuff of urban legend.

Children and their parents informed park personnel, who were at first skeptical – until they witnessed snack-time themselves. Traps were set and the pair soon imprisoned.

But then the park's overseers faced the problem of what to do with a couple of fast-growing alligators. An idea was hatched, and, on the hill facing the lake from the west side of the park, a pen was constructed, with a small pond and a few rocks. The alligators, at least, could view their former home, with its duck population, from their new digs.

Later, they would be joined on the hill by a pair of lions (named Romeo and Juliet), a troop of monkeys, fowl ranging from noisy guineas to showy peacocks to pushy pigeons taking advantage of the park-provided food intended for the official residents. Eventually, Ole Diamond, the elephant generally credited with being the catalyst of today's first-rate zoological garden, would join them.

But, in my family, Kenneth and Maynard, two scaley Florida fugitives named for their rescuers, were the true founders of the zoo.

~~~~~~~~~~

THOUGH THE naming of the alligators may have been unconventional, distinctive names followed Burlington tradition: Most of the men sported handles beyond what was on their birth certificates, at least in the 1930s. That was certainly true of my parents' male friends.

There was Corky and his brother, Wheeler. They owned Moulton Brothers Amoco station. There was a guy called Babe and another who went by Cooner. One of my uncles answered to Buster. My dad was known as Fats. Until my mother put a stop to it, I was called Little Fats.

There was Smut, and his son, Slim. The operator of the movie theater was called Bunny. There was a man who went by Son, and a bootlegger called Cotton. The husband of one longtime Sunday-school teacher – and a permanent subject of church-wide prayers – was known as Sparky. The woman who played the organ at church was married to a man called Bugs. Ottie was the older brother of one of my mother's best friends.

The gunsmith who operated in a garage down the alley from my grandparents, a Cherokee, was known to everyone as Indian.

And there was the legendary Dodie, who had left home while a teen-ager to wander around the country, riding the rails. Periodically, when a freight brought him back to the area, he would show up at one of the gas-station hangouts to bring his old friends up to date on his adventures. Then he would hit the road again.

Once, when my dad was telling a story of his youth, he mentioned a man who attended our church whose last name was Hockenjos. What was his nickname? I asked.

"Didn't need one," my dad said, implying that a surname like that was differentiation enough. There was certainly no problem with his being confused with another church regular, a fixture of the gospel quartet featured at Sunday-night services. His name was Ailshie – pronounced ale-shy. I never heard either referred to by their given names.

There were others who were nicknameless. Burlington's Esso station was owned by Mayford Mitchell, his first name distinctive enough. Something wrong with your car? "See if Mayford can help" was all that was needed. Everyone knew whom you were talking about.

My grandfather on my mother's side didn't need a nickname either, since his given name was Boss Lones. But no one called him Boss except his wife – he went by his initials, B.L.

The nicknaming didn't seem to carry over to females. In most cases the given names were enough. My grandmother, Boss's wife, was Etta. My mother's circle included Ola Mae, Rosalee, Venita and Lela.

Sometimes, as with Hockenjos and Ailshie, the family name was all that was needed. The last name of the woman who lived next door to Boss and Etta was Stover. And, as far as we knew that was the only name she had. Fixing dinner, my grandmother might send me next door to "see if Stover can loan me a cup of sugar."

In the late 1930s, while he was still single, before he got on with Alcoa, my dad ran the Texaco station about two blocks away from where Corky and Wheeler operated. Mayford's Esso station was between the two. The Texaco was at the intersection of Rutledge Pike and Holston Drive, the last stop heading northeast out of town. And, like Mayford's and the Moulton Brothers' and other service stations of the era, it was a gathering place for neighborhood men.

As such, it figured into many of Dad's tales. When I was a child, there were regular Sunday-night gatherings after church when my parents' group would get together for what they called "fellowships." Someone would make a run to the Krispy Kreme doughnut operation on Magnolia Avenue (open all night, even on Sunday) and they would then gather at our house, or at the home of Corky and Venita, or at Mayford and Lela's. (The latter sticks in my memory because Lela kept her Christmas decorations up year-round.) Then the coffee and reminiscence would flow.

Mayford was tall and lanky, with a booming voice and a self-deprecating manner. Corky and Wheeler were quick to laugh, and all three were expert at getting my dad, the laconic one, to tell his part of the stories.

One tale involved a late-night visit to a sidetracked boxcar and a stolen case of mayonnaise, the joke being that no one could remember the "why." When Mayford asked my dad, he just nodded toward Corky. "It was his idea," he said.

And there was a story of after-dark fishing in the Holston River at the end of Ruggles Ferry Pike, the ferry being closed for the day and tied up on the other side. A carload of teen-agers came flying down the road and ran into the river at the spot where the ferry was normally anchored. As the car slowly sank into the shallow water they scrambled out, my dad and his friends looking on. Climbing up the bank, one of the wet revelers wondered indignantly why there was no sign warning of the stream. My dad's answer, as Mayford recalled, was: "A fella can't see a river, I don't see how he could see a sign."

One story that Dad told me decades later provided my introduction to Cooner. Early one warm evening, Dad said, he and Cooner were sitting out front of the Texaco station, swapping stories, when a bootlegger of their acquaintance pulled in.

"He had a sack full of quarters and half-dollars that he wanted to change into bills," Dad said. "I couldn't help him and steered him to the five-and-dime up the street."

"I guess he was in a hurry because he left the motor running in his car. When he was out of sight, Cooner jumped into the Ford and drove off."

What did the bootlegger do when he saw what happened, I wanted to know.

"He cussed and kicked for a while. Finally, he called somebody to come get him. They drove off, headed out Rutledge Pike."

What happened to Cooner, I asked.

"I don't know," Dad said. "I never saw him again."

~~~~~~~~~~~

BY THE TIME I started school we were living on the side of the ridge that formed Burlington's southern boundary. Our house was on Selma Avenue, one block down the hill from Skyline Drive, which ran along the top of the ridge. Skyline defined the ridge – the north side, toward the business district, was more prosperous; the south side fell away into pockets of dilapidated residences, woods, and an overgrown field of several acres that was known as the Hollow.

My dad and Papaw Monday had built our house after Dad bought the lot from a man who had started construction but had gotten no farther than a one-story, concrete-block foundation. Dad had put in the house's flooring and covered it with insulation and tarpaper, providing a roof for the basement. We moved in while he and Papaw built the house above our temporary home. A few years later, they added two more rooms and another bathroom.

A Burlington fixture named Frank helped out with the more physical labor – mixing concrete with a hoe and hauling wheelbarrow loads of dirt and bags of cement. He was, Mom would say, "a little slow in his thinking," but was kept busy with manual jobs throughout Burlington. His mother, a tall, long-striding woman, did the same, cleaning and taking in ironing.

Every morning Frank would head into Burlington looking for work. When Dad needed him, he would drive to Henderlight's Feed and Seed where Frank, if someone hadn't already hired him, would be sitting out front. At some point, Frank fixated on a particular cap that my dad sometimes wore that always struck him as funny. When I would see him, even years later, he would ask if Dad was still wearing that hat. I would tell him yes, and he would laugh.

Another neighborhood woman who took in ironing was better known – at least to the kids – for her story-telling skill. Miz Lusby's house was a short walk from our place, on the edge of the Hollow. She was, according to word around the neighborhood, a bit of a witch. Because of that reputation, and because of the tales she told, she was popular with us.

During warm weather, after supper when twilight was deepening, she could often be found sitting on her front porch in a rocking chair that appeared to be even older than she was. And often a half-dozen or so kids would be gathered around, waiting for one of her stories.

She liked to scare us with accounts of in-house wakes, the honoree stretched out in his or her coffin in the parlor, mourners gathered around in the dim light of candles or lanterns. The memories that were shared by the mourners would invariably involve a violent act, sometimes following a mysterious night-time chase. One such chase, one of the more memorable, involved a "panter."

Panters – panthers or cougars – were a particular favorite of Miz Lusby. Though they had not been spotted officially in East Tennessee for decades, she was sure they were still around. "A panter is smart," she would say. "He learns how to stay away from human beings, only coming out at night to raid a barn or a pig sty, grabbing a baby pig or a newborn calf for his supper."

So, according to her, panthers were responsible for the mysterious disappearance of farm animals, or, she would imply, somebody's dog. "They wouldn't mess with cats," she contended. "Some people say it's because they're too small, not worth messing with. But the real reason is because they're cats, too. They're kin, so the panter don't mess with 'em."

And, she liked to emphasize, "A panter's cry is just like a baby's – if you ever hear one in the middle of the night, it'll sound just like a little baby crying." Of course we all knew the sound of the neighborhood tomcats' nighttime wailing, so we could easily imagine the sound of a panter. And, just to make sure we understood what she was talking about, she would sometimes demonstrate, executing a long, drawn-out cry that sounded just like a baby.

Miz Lusby was a "widow woman". Her husband, according to neighborhood lore, had disappeared not too long after they were married, then turned up dead in Texas. Some said he had been shot. Miz Lusby had lived alone ever since, with a dog and a cat or two. No one ever said anything about how she survived, except through her ironing and sewing. And she had a garden during spring and summer. We weren't interested in such details. We only wanted to hear her tales. Sometimes, one of us would ask about how to keep a panter away. She would say that it didn't always work, but there was a spell you could use. She would then tease us. If we could find her a black-cat bone she would tell us how to use it. "It takes some practice, and it don't always work," she would insist, "but it's your best chance."

Once, Earl Presley brought her a small bone he'd found, claiming that he was sure it came from a black cat. She took one look and said, "No, that's from a possum."

About the time I got a decent bicycle and was getting old enough to start scoffing at her stories, she delivered the tale that topped them all. She delivered it so believably that I forgot my recently acquired skepticism and sat up and listened.

She had heard a panter the night before, and it was so close, she said, it had to be in the Hollow. Most of us had spent time in the Hollow – it was full of blackberry bushes as well as rabbit tobacco and hidden spots for smoking it.

Eyes widened as she demonstrated the panter's cry, and provided details of her two cats trying to get out of her house when the wailing began. "They were wanting to go join it, I reckon," she said. "I didn't sleep another wink, I can tell you."

Then, a few days later, at the height of blackberry season, I saw Miz Lusby in the Hollow, busy filling a pan with berries. She had the entire place to herself, all the kids staying away lest there be a panter present.

~~~~~~~~~~

A COUPLE of blocks away from Miz Lusby's, at the corner of Skyline and Fern Street, stood Holbert's Cash Grocery, one of those neighborhood spots that were common before supermarkets and fast-food behemoths drove them out of business. You could get a bottle of milk or a loaf of bread or a can of beans without having to drive to the business district. A chili dog could be had for a dime. Add a bag of chips and a cold drink and you had a meal that was long on taste if short on nutrition.

I would take whatever empty soft-drink bottles I could round up and turn them in for two cents each. If I had enough empties, I had the price of a cold Grapette.

But the bottles had to be damage-free. The man who ran Holbert's – I guess it was Mr. Holbert himself – would sometimes refuse to accept a soft-drink bottle, pointing out a small chip that he said made it worthless. Once when I was in his store, he caught a kid trying to cheat him out of a penny gumball. I don't remember the details – it might have been a penny-sized slug. He told the perp that if he ever saw him in his store again he would call the police.

His attitude was understandable given his clientele, mostly kids, many from the wrong side of the ridge, where several of the houses still featured tar-papered exteriors. I sometimes delivered the afternoon paper on that side of the ridge, helping out Earl Presley, who had the route. Scruffy dogs could make the job chancy. Collection days often meant payment in pennies – if there was payment at all.

It was the neighborhood of a couple of boys I first met at Holbert's – Foxx and Crowder. I didn't know them from Fair Garden School; they apparently had decided to forego that part of education.

I never knew where Crowder called home, but Foxx lived a few doors beyond Holbert's. And he joined us when we decided to dig a hideout into the side of a hill in the woods between our house and Holbert's. There we could escape younger siblings and the neighborhood's nosy old ladies.

A meeting at the hideout featured a lot of big talk, and Foxx would sometimes demonstrate how to smoke cigarettes. I don't remember any of us taking up his dare on the fags, but I do remember that he confessed that his old man was in prison for selling marijuana.

Of course he had to explain what marijuana was. He went on to helpfully tell us how his dad would empty half of the tobacco out of a Lucky Strike and replace it with pot. He was caught, Foxx said, with an entire carton of Luckies that he had meticulously loaded.

Once I started high school the hideout was forgotten and I only saw Foxx occasionally. He and Crowder were boxing fans and I sometimes ran into them at Golden Gloves matches at the Jacobs Building in Chilhowee Park.

But the last time I heard anything about the pair was several years later, when I was living in Kentucky, working for The Louisville Times newspaper.

I had picked up a copy of The Knoxville Journal and discovered a story that featured Foxx and Crowder and a spot on the Holston River a couple miles east of Burlington. There had been a middle-of-the-night gathering in a wooded section alongside the river. I knew the spot – I had camped there when I was in the Boy Scouts.

There was a bonfire and a lot of alcohol. Crowder had either jumped or was thrown into the river. He didn't surface – his body was found the next day.

I called a Burlington acquaintance for details. "There were quite a few of them partying," he told me. "And they'd been going since the middle of the afternoon. It was well after midnight when he went in."

"I've heard," he added, "that they think Foxx may have shoved him in, either just horsing around or on-purpose."

Given the alcohol, the time of the night, the reputations – and rap sheets – of those present, the authorities ended their investigation, and Crowder's death was ruled an accident.

By then, the site of Holbert's, which had closed decades earlier, was a trash-strewn lot.

~~~~~~~~~~

TROOP 15, Boy Scouts of America, met on Thursday nights at Kirkwood Presbyterian Church on McCalla Avenue in the heart of Burlington. The church building was small, but there was an adequate meeting room in the basement, and more importantly, a grassy back area perfect for games of "Pitch Up and Smear."

I can't remember the objective of the game, but it involved a football that was thrown into the air, with everyone scrambling to catch it. The lucky Scout was then susceptible to a "smearing" by the others unless he could get the ball to someone else. There must have been some kind of scoring system. Understandably, not everyone present wanted to participate.

Most of us were veterans of such neighborhood games. But one of the kids, not a Burlington resident, expressed an intellectual skepticism to the game's "point." His name was Richard, and his dad would drop him off for the meetings. He lived in Park City, the next neighborhood to the west. Afterward, we would gather in the church's meeting room with the scoutmaster, Jimmy Coppock, presiding. The church might have been modest, but, thanks to Mr. Coppock, the troop enjoyed a certain prestige in the Great Smoky Mountain Council of the Scouts. Mr. Coppock, a postman by day, was a longtime fixture with the organization and holder of a Silver Beaver Award, one of Scouting's top honors.

Though the meeting place was Presbyterian, the troop membership reflected the community, drawing from McCalla Avenue Baptist, across the street, from Burlington Methodist, a couple of blocks away, and from other churches in the area.

The troop shared ownership with another troop of a cabin on Chilhowee Mountain in the Smokies. The cabin – one long room with a porch that ran its entire length – was equipped with rustic bunk beds, a fireplace, and a wood-burning cook stove. A spring just above it on the mountain provided water. During warm weather we would spend three or four weekends there.

At that time, the late 1950s, that part of the mountain was serviced by a barely usable dirt road. At one point in the 1920s, we were told, on the Knoxville side of the peak there had been a resort hotel called Dupont Springs. Sometimes we would hike up there and scout around the spot where it had supposedly stood.

Our cabin was on the side facing Sevierville to the southeast, about two-thirds of the way to the top. It was well off the dirt road, barely visible in the winter when the trees were bare. There was only one other usable cabin in the area, owned by the couple that had donated the land for the Scout facility.

The road, most of the time, was passable by car or truck, but we always hiked up, complaining most of the way, badgering Mr. Coppock with distance questions. No matter how many miles remained, his stock answer became a running joke. When asked how much farther, he always said: "Mile, mile and a half, two miles."

Sometimes, those of us who were more experienced, who had his trust, would be allowed to hike up a creek, scrambling through the woods in an attempt to get to the cabin ahead of those using the road. Once, on a dare, Ray Merritt and I toted a watermelon, along with our usual gear, the entire three and a half miles up the road. Mr. Coppock saw to it that we shared the melon with the others even though we pointed out that none of them had volunteered to help carry it.

Later, I figured out that I could lighten my load by simplifying my diet. The only food I carried was a package or two of wieners, a loaf of bread and a jar of mustard. No cooking pans, no eating utensils. All I needed was a sharpened stick and a fire to make my hot dogs, which I ate for every meal. Mr. Coppock told me that though my thought process was admirable, I was a bad example for the younger boys.

But Mr. Coppock's greatest lesson to us came when the question of religion arose on one of the trips. I don't remember how it began, but someone started talking about the difference between being a Baptist and being a Methodist or Presbyterian. Obviously, being dipped under the water was scarier than being sprinkled, so Baptist was a tougher religion. Or something along those lines.

Richard wasn't participating in the argument, and someone finally asked him what religion he was. He simply said he wasn't any of those. One of the kids pressed him, and Mr. Coppock then stepped in, explaining that Richard was Jewish and what that meant.

As I remember, there were a couple of shrugs and that was the end of it. We all took pride in the fact that Troop 15 had its own cabin in the mountains – something that most other troops did not have. But now, at least for most of us, we had something else that set us apart: We had a Jewish member.

Years later, I was told by someone from Richard's neighborhood that the scoutmaster of that neighborhood troop would not allow Jewish members. That would explain why he joined Troop 15, far enough away that his dad had to drive him to meetings.

~~~~~~~~~~~

MY BOY SCOUT days coincided with my move from Fair Garden School to the seventh grade, a move that in many ways was more than a mere move. It was a leap. I went from the neighborhood atmosphere of Fair Garden to Park Junior High School, several miles west toward downtown.

That meant a ride on the city bus to and from school, either via Magnolia or McCalla avenues. True, most of the kids who were my classmates in grades one through six were still with me. But there were new faces, too, from different parts of town, primarily Park City and the area along the river just east of downtown.

And there were more technical offerings such as woodshop and mechanical drawing – even a plastics class. The grades were seventh, eighth, and for some, ninth. I noticed fairly early that a few of the students were much older. A couple even drove cars to school. The primer-gray early-'50s Mercury that a kid named Julian drove was particularly cool.

But the real eye-opener came about the third week of my seventh-grade year. I had noticed that the boy who sat behind me in homeroom was older. His surname was Young, and he told me he lived on Hill Avenue above the Tennessee River. That neighborhood consisted of run-down Victorian houses, many of which had been divided into apartments; a few years later it was bulldozed out of existence in an urban-renewal effort.

One morning about 8:40, just after the pledge of allegiance to the flag, two policemen entered, had a quick conversation with the teacher, came down my aisle, and led Mr. Young out. We never saw him again.

A month or so later, the south end of the school was shaken during third period by an explosion. A quick trip into the hall revealed water streaming from the boys' bathroom. Later, we learned that someone had dropped a cherry bomb (waterproof fuse) down one of the toilets.

The result proved popular – exploding toilets became regular occurrences, finally leading to a patrolling policeman.

Uniformed officers also joined us on the Magnolia Avenue bus after school. Their presence became necessary after a game developed among those occupying the back seat, which went all the way across the vehicle. A handful of the boys discovered that they could push on the bus sides and squeeze the kids who were in the middle.

After the second time that a bus window was popped out by the pushing, a cop became a regular rider.

When I took wood shop, I noticed that some of the boys were making Y-shaped sling shots. Then one of the older students shaped a wooden pistol, rigging it up for rubber bands. The weaponry development soon escalated with technical advice from an older brother. The result was a zip gun capable of firing a .22 bullet. The gunsmith, too, was escorted out by policemen and not seen in the hallways again.

In the eighth grade, I became involved in the Black & Gold, a mimeographed newsletter that appeared sporadically and was shepherded by my homeroom teacher. In hindsight a crime column would have been popular, but I doubt if the idea would have met with the principal's approval.

Eventually, some of the troublemakers started answering to a skinny kid named Harrison, who had seen a few James Cagney-George Raft features and adopted their movie characters as role models. He had leadership ability (he was probably at least three years older than most of us) and soon had a half-dozen followers.

Harrison and a couple of his lieutenants began stopping seventh graders in the hall, guiding them to a quiet corner and asking "What would you do if someone just walked up and slugged you in the jaw?"

The wide-eyed response was usually along the lines of, "I don't know."

Then the "insurance" racket would be explained. "We can protect you from that kind of thing, and all you have to do is pay us a quarter a week." (This was the late 1950s, when the school lunch was only 50 cents.) The business started off well and soon became the subject of lunchroom whispers and nervous glances in Harrison's direction.

But then Harrison made a serious mistake. During the mid-day break, while the lunchroom was crowded, he approached Slack, one of my Burlington buddies, with his proposition. Slack had an immediate response – he cold-cocked Harrison. Harrison became a laughing stock, his entrepreneurial attempt at an end.

~~~~~~~~~~

THE KITCHEN TABLE of our house on Selma Avenue was Gossip Central, with my mother the mistress of ceremonies. The other participants varied, with a half dozen or so regulars. The subjects were the peccadillos – both real and rumored – of most everyone else in the neighborhood and at McCalla Avenue Baptist Church, where we were members.

If I was quiet, seemingly absorbed in a game or a book, I could catch the gist of the conversation. Obviously, I had developed a penchant for journalism at an early age. One frequent subject was a family from our church, a family that included 12 children. The patriarch was not popular with the kitchen-table group.

He had, according to my mother, insisted that he was going to father a dozen kids. He was successful, though the ordeals of birthing the youngest three or four "almost killed his wife."

Usually my mother, a stickler for education, would add a knowing, "Why, he can't even read or write." I had no reason to doubt that, as he made his living by sporadic manual-labor jobs – scuffling – with the family frequent benefactors of the church's community-outreach efforts.

It didn't occur to me until years later that many adults couldn't read or write. True, I knew some who had never learned to drive a car. But I never considered that the insurmountable hurdle for many might have been the written driver's test.

In the grocery line once, when I was impatiently squirming because it was taking so long, my grandmother quieted me by whispering that the woman in front, an acquaintance, was having a problem with the prices because she could not read.

When I was in high school, my sister told me about a friend's father who was illiterate. Retired, he was taking an adult-education course to try to rectify his problem.

Later, after professionals began to understand and diagnose dyslexia, it became obvious that illiteracy often could be traced to that affliction. That, his daughter was convinced, was her dad's problem. Whatever the reason for his not being able to read and write, she said, "He always provided for us."

Nowadays, of course, dyslexia is addressed in school, with special attention. Other learning disabilities – attention-deficit disorder, for example – are also diagnosed and addressed.

A friend and I were discussing the issue, and how it was basically unknown when we were in elementary school in the 1950s, when he mentioned one of his theories. Many tradesmen – he specifically mentioned carpenters – probably were so afflicted, and that's one reason they were attracted to their vocation, where reading was not required. There is probably some basis for that observation.

Looking back, I remember an occasional episode that demonstrated the truth of the time, and one that happened after I had learned about dyslexia. I had contracted with a friend of the family who was in his 60s to help move some stuff to the dump.

Years ago, I had begun to suspect he couldn't read, as there had been a couple of episodes involving fuse boxes and printed instructions.

In this case, I was driving, and when I pulled onto one street near our destination, he proudly read the sign naming the street.

It was a two-name drive; he nailed the first word, but mis-read the second. When I corrected him, he just said, "That's what I meant." The episode and his response, I'm sure, had often been repeated.

My younger brother had problems in school that were later, after he was well out of school, diagnosed as dyslexia-based. He had compensated by being a class clown, a role that led to frequent visits to the principal's office.

Like many others, he was passed along, moved up a grade by teachers and administrators who had no idea what the problem was.

When we were adults and I would ask if he wanted to join me on a research-run to the library, he would always beg off. And he had a perplexing habit, at family gatherings, of immediately bringing up a subject that I had cautioned him not to mention. Somehow, despite his handicap, he managed to accumulate most of the credits needed for a bachelor of arts degree.

He struggled most of his life finding and holding a job, finally finding success by creating a position involving photography. Auto-focus cameras solved his problem.

Most members of my mother's gossip circle attended McCalla Avenue Baptist, which meant that many of the conversations centered on church activity. Mom sang in the choir and led a Sunday School class. Dad was a deacon.

Up until my late teens, I was a regular attendee of morning and evening services as well as Sunday School and Training Union and the annual Vacation Bible Schools and week-long revivals. Occasionally there were dinners on the grounds, too, with fried chicken and potato salad and deviled eggs in infinite variety.

While I was enthusiastic about the dinners, I was a reluctant attendee of the regular services and the revivals. Given Mom and Dad's roles, my siblings and I had no choice but to be in church when they were. Decisions to skip the service in favor of the soda counter at the nearby Greenlee's Drug Store were made risky by Mom's position in the choir. She scanned the pews to see that we were not only present, but upright and awake.

And staying awake could be a problem. The church was large enough – more than 1,000 members – that ritual took precedence over spirit, at least on Sunday mornings. Longtime members had sat through hundreds of sermons, delivered by dozens of preachers. Many were prone to dozing. There was one lanky member, habitué of the rear of the auditorium, who was well-known to me and my friends. He would nod off, his head would drift backward and his Adam's apple would bob with his breathing. We found the sight amusing, a diversion that kept us awake.

Another diversion, usually occurring only at evening services, involved an older choir member who would be moved to dance from her seat in the loft down to the front of the altar, choir robe swirling. We didn't know whether to laugh or run.

Reluctant though I was about the sermonizing, I didn't mind Vacation Bible School. My dad, who worked the second shift at Alcoa, was available in the mornings and would be called on for VBS, usually put in charge of crafts for the boys.

I would be drafted to help, loading pieces of plywood into the station wagon, along with the saws and files that would be used to cut them into animal shapes. They would then be decorated with colored popcorn. Sometimes, the end product would actually resemble a chicken or a rabbit – or something nightmarishly in-between. Afterward, I would wield a broom as we cleaned up the scattered popcorn.

By the time I was 12 or 13, plywood animals didn't hold much interest for my age group. Crafts hour degenerated into popcorn battles, saws and files becoming dangerous weapons.

As I became more hindrance than help, Dad enlisted another deacon. Boomer, as I'll call him here, was an automobile mechanic, and he had an idea. With several boxes of old carburetors, he brought in screwdrivers, wrenches, and a can of kerosene and shop rags for cleaning. He showed us how to disassemble the carbs, how to clean all the parts with kerosene, and how to put them back together. We worked on single-barrels, then two-barrels, and, finally, at week's end, four-barrels. There were a lot of greasy fingers and oil-stained clothes, but no more popcorn battles.

But as I grew older and bought my own car, with its own carburetor, I moved away from active church participation, eventually working a part-time job downtown. It was then that I started taking note of street preachers. Knoxville had its share, most of them active on Saturdays on Market Square. Their breathy buildups and sing-song deliveries were fascinating, at least as a lunchtime diversion. One young man who was particularly entertaining was adept at leaping into the air at particular points during his sermons, jumping just as he slapped his Bible against his hand, his timing precise.

After I graduated college and changed jobs, moving from city to city, other Bible thumpers caught my attention. In downtown Dallas dueling preachers worked a particularly busy street corner. One would sermonize for a while, the other looking on in disgust. When the first ran out of steam, the second would start, his competitor watching with a disdainful look.

Atlanta featured several of note. There was a woman, part of a group that wore white robes, who would smoothly segue from preaching to singing, her "sisters" joining in on the chorus. But downtown Atlanta's best as spectacle was an African-American man who worked Woodruff Park at lunchtime. He carried a guitar slung over his shoulder, though I never saw him play it. What made him interesting was his "shadow." At some point, a young white man had decided to follow him closely and mimic his movements, making fun of him. The shadow became enough of a problem that a third person joined in: an Atlanta policeman who made sure the shadow didn't get too close.

After I had moved back to Knoxville in 1994, I encountered another lay preacher, with a technique I had never seen before. I was sitting at a downtown traffic light when I heard a voice praising God. Despite being at shout volume, the voice seemed to be disembodied, but the message was clear: If we all didn't change our ways, we were going to Hell.

Finally, I spotted the source of the sermon. The driver of a truck was shouting his message to everyone waiting on the red light – preaching to the air.

Though I found street preachers intriguing, I had long ago decided I didn't want middlemen between me and my maker, epiphany coming when I was middle-school age and still attending the church of my childhood. One of the ministers was a slick, charismatic character with a wife and five children. His spouse, who sat next to my mother in the choir, was the butt of his jokes when he made his reports to the congregation on Sunday mornings. And, I overheard my mother tell her friends, she would whisper funny asides in response, using language not suited for church.

But one afternoon as Mom and her friends gossiped, I overheard a different tale about the minister. It seemed that he was having an affair with a church member, also married. I didn't hear much detail – one of Mom's friends noticed that I was in the room, and I was quickly sent outside.

The next Sunday, the minister and his wife were not present at either service. The word quickly spread that he had resigned and that he and his family were leaving Knoxville. Over the next couple of weeks I picked up bits and pieces of the story, but I was too involved in my own shenanigans to pay much attention.

The years passed, the neighborhood changed, and the church merged with another congregation. I was living in Kansas

City at the time. Mom and Dad were active in the new church for a while, until the fundamentalists started taking over the Southern Baptist Convention. My parents were both strong believers in formal education, and the mail-order degrees held by the new faction appalled them.

Eventually the new church called a new preacher, a fundamentalist whose education was, as far as my mother was concerned, seriously lacking. She soon was at loggerheads with him and he fired her from the Sunday School class she had been leading for years, even sending a young minister-in-training to suggest that she not tell anyone why she was no longer teaching. She told him that if any of the women asked about her absence she wouldn't lie. Eventually, she and my dad quit attending.

My parents knew everyone in that area of Knoxville, and my mother, never shy, wielded considerable influence. The new preacher – she had taken to calling him Pope John – decided he needed her back in attendance. He began regular visitations at their house.

His entreaties only angered her. Finally, she told him that if she came to church it would be to call for his ouster. Under Southern Baptist Convention rules, any church member can call for a vote about a minister at any service; if there is a second, the vote must be held then and there. Her threat was sufficient, and Pope John didn't come around anymore.

Years later, at my father's funeral, I spoke with many of his old friends from the old church, the shade-tree mechanics he talked cars with, fellow machinists, the neighbors he helped when their vehicles wouldn't start. But I didn't see Boomer.

Later, talking about the crowd with my brother and sister, I mentioned his absence. My sister looked over at me. I guess you didn't hear, she said: He committed suicide years ago.

My look of surprise led her to explain. Boomer had had a drinking problem, a problem that became worse with the discovery years earlier that his wife was involved with one of the church's ministers.

License to Roam

Tales of the Midway – Playing Santa Claus – Food fights and creative cussing – Rampage on the bread route – A late-night trip to jail – Killian's '51 Ford

~~~~~~~~~~~

BY THE TIME I reached high-school age, my familiarity with the fairgrounds across from my grandparents' house had led to an interest in working the annual East Tennessee Agricultural and Industrial Fair that took place late summer of every year. And that interest eventually led to a brief career as a carny.

When I was about 12, my mother pointed out that my grandparents' backyard, accessed by the alley, was perfect for parking cars at fair time. It was only a couple hundred yards from one of the main gates. I could charge the premium rate, which at the time was 50 cents. The yard would hold 10 or 12 vehicles, depending on how I crammed them in. If there was turnover, I might make as much as $18 or $20 per day. And, for a 12-year-old in the mid-1950s, that was a lot of money.

Once the yard was full, and it was dark enough for the Midway to be running at full tilt, my friends would drop by and we would sneak into the fair. We had a couple of difficult, over-the-fence routes we used until we discovered a much easier way to get past the ticket-takers.

The closest gate was the entry for vendors. One night a couple of us were standing outside the gate, on the opposite side from the ticket booth, when a milk truck approached from the inside. We quickly realized that when it started through the gate it would hide us from the ticket-takers. A few steps and we were inside, soon to be lost in the crowd.

Hanging out in the fairgrounds with friends who manned community-club food concessions, we took to calling ourselves carnies.

By the time I was in high school, I had learned that one of my grandparents' neighbors owned concession set-ups that he operated with various carnival companies. So, a couple of weeks before the fair was due to start, I knocked on Mr. Bradley's door. He asked if I had a food-worker's card. Because of my other, year-round part-time job – delivering bread for Swan's Bakery on Sundays – I had the proper credentials. I was hired.

Mr. Bradley's entry-level position for a neophyte like me was the popcorn stand at the zoo, atop a hill on the western edge of the fairgrounds. Unfortunately, it was quite a distance from the real action, where Gooding's Million Dollar Midway was set up. But, he said, once it got dark and zoo visitation ceased, I could close up and move down the hill to help at a duck-pond game of chance that he owned.

The duck pond was operated by the Roback brothers, who I knew from East High School. The youngest, Farouk (Frookie to his friends), was my age and a partner in various school escapades that I had been involved in. At one time, as I recall, he held the school record for suspensions.

The duck pond was set up at a prime site, at the entrance to the tunnel that went under Magnolia Avenue to the fairground's south side, where the midway operated. Revelers entering the tunnel were passing from the livestock exhibits – rambunctious bulls, snorting pigs and preening roosters – to the fantasy world of the Million Dollar Midway, with its colorful lights, glamorous burlesque, games of chance, freak shows and exotic characters.

Frookie, already a legend at East High, was hard at work polishing his image. Expanding on the standard "Come in, you win," he had developed his own patter to lure the unsuspecting to the duck-pond game.

Affecting a speech impediment, he would yell "Free, free, free," then after a pause, "One for a dime, free for a quarter."

Another favorite played to the macho tendencies of the teen-aged males enjoying a date night. Spotting such a couple, he would yell, "Hey, buddy, bring your sister over here and win her a prize." Often, there would be a dirty look and a, "She's not my sister, she's my girl." Of course, then Frookie had him.

On the other side of the tunnel, marking the beginning of the Midway, was an "I Got It" game. It was manned by another East High classmate, Donny Anderson. Where the rest of us were would-be carnies, Donny was for real. He was, as he says, "born into the carnival" and spent more than three dozen years traveling the country, pitching games of chance, selling "lemon shakeups," operating rides, and eventually running his own full-blown operation.

Anderson's parents, Norman and Marguerite, owned rides and games, and they traveled from their Knoxville home every year, late spring to early fall. Donny was born in 1943 at an Army base in Kentucky just before his dad shipped out. His mother's father, Earl Burkhart, saw an opportunity and converted his carnival concession. "He had one of those moon-picture set-ups where he would take your picture sitting on the moon," Donny recalled several years later for a story I was doing on his experiences. "He left off the moon and was taking pictures of the soldiers as they shipped out.

"As soon as my dad came back, we were out on the road operating Bingo games. We had a travel trailer, a Spartan Manor, and I remember in Kentucky – this was in the early 1950s – for some reason it was against the law to travel with those things on Sundays, which was our travel day.

"My dad would be several miles ahead driving one of the semis, and Mom would be driving the car towing the trailer with me and my little brother Joe. And we would get pulled over and escorted to state police headquarters.

"They'd let us hook up for electricity and then Joe and I would go inside the station and bother the policemen in hopes that they would get tired of us and let us go. Sometimes it worked.

"Dad taught me how to call Bingo – B-7, I-16, N-42 – and I was the caller by the time I was 12 or 13. Later, when several states decided Bingo was a lottery, we had to convert it to a game of skill. So you tossed rubber balls onto a board with holes cut out until you lined them up. That was called "I Got It."

"Dad kept expanding, and finally we were Anderson's Greater Shows. We would start in March, fixing and painting, and then in May, we'd do what are called festivals, smaller shows in towns like Corbin, Kentucky.

"July 4 marked the beginning of the carnival season. After that it was county fair to regional fair to state fair until early October.

"Knoxville was always the date after Labor Day. Gooding's Million Dollar Midway was the contractor and their show before was the Indiana State Fair in Indianapolis. The date following Knoxville was the Tennessee State Fair in Nashville, so Knoxville got one of the bigger Midways designed for the state fairs."

Knoxville's fair usually marked a homecoming for the Andersons. And an opportunity for Donny to show off for his schoolmates. "I was proficient at all the games because I had been doing them since I was big enough to walk. So I would win at everything and my friends would love it. At least until the game owners wouldn't let me play anymore.

"I was just a kid, and I investigated everything. I watched the tattoo artist work. And I checked out the sideshow – the sword swallowers, the girl with no head, Emmitt the alligator man and Priscilla the monkey lady, who had hair all over her body. Everything was quasi-scientific – the guy explaining the attractions was called a 'lecturer.' By the way, Emmitt and Priscilla were married and had a child who was perfectly normal."

When Donny was older, he and his dad became involved in Knoxville's Golden Gloves boxing program, and he fought as a middleweight through high school, before becoming ring announcer for local tournaments. He was a natural, having several seasons' experience using a microphone to lure customers into I Got It games.

"There were only certain attractions that could use a microphone," Donny says. "You had to be considerate of nearby games. In fact, there was an arbitrator with Gooding who would go around making sure nobody was drowning out their neighbors."

His boxing skills sometimes came in handy on the Midway. Once, Donny returned to his car, parked outside the burlesque show, to find three locals standing on the hood trying to see over the tent wall.

"I decked one of 'em, and they took off," he says. The most likely trouble spots, however, had to do with the clowns who sat over a tank of water and dared participants to dump them into the tank with a baseball thrown well enough to strike a bullseye.

"They were called Bozo Bills, and they were the original insult artists. Usually they would pick out a particular physical feature and then ride that to heat up the thrower so he would keep paying out his dollar for three throws. If the guy had a big nose, it would be 'Is that your nose or are you eating a banana?' or maybe they would comment on him being skinny or fat.

"Often at closing time, a bunch of us would have to go escort the Bozo because one of the throwers would be waiting to settle up. We'd surround the Bozo, maybe talk to the customer, get right in his face, and change his mind."

If there was trouble on the Midway, the cry that let the other workers know that help was needed was, "Hey Rube."

"That generally meant there was a fight, and you tried to get right to it," Donny says. "You'd find the ring-leader and get him away from the crowd. We always had plenty of uniformed security, off-duty officers. Because of that and because of the communication, we made sure the Midway was always a very safe place."

"Hey Rube" is just one piece of a distinct carnival language. "If you wanted to talk with someone so that other people couldn't understand what you were saying," Donny explains, "you'd 'crack carny'. You'd take the first letter of a word, add iz and then put the rest of the word back on. For example: 'Lizets gizo to the cizook hizouse', which is 'Let's go to the cook house' – the tent where the workers ate. Then there's one of my favorites, 'gizoonie', someone who's goofy.

"Another common term is 'bally'. The bally talker is the person working the microphone.

"I still remember one bally line from the motodrome show: 'It's the dome of death where they rip, ride and drive those high-powered racing motorcycles.' It has a great rhythm.

"One of Gooding's best bally talkers was a guy named Gary, who worked the burlesque show. He got 10 percent off the top, so it was in his best interest to fill up the tent. He'd always start by drawing the customers' attention to a half-dollar – getting them to move in close so the tip – the carnival term for crowd – didn't block the Midway. Then he'd bring the girls out one by one with a little introduction, usually full of double entendres. After they were all on the stage they'd do a short number and go back inside, hopefully with a large part of the audience following."

Gary's spiel included detailed descriptions of each dancer's specialty, and, though the girls might change year to year, the specialty was just transferred to the new dancer. One memorable perennial was, "Tondalaya, and her famous dance of the Kookanoognas."

The Midway also included another review, an all-African-American show that was reputed to be hotter and raunchier than the white burlesque. One of the more famous was Nate Groves' Harlem Nights, which was part of the Knoxville Midway for several years.

"They would have the Midnight Ramble," Donny says, "which was when the music got hotter, the jokes raunchier and the costumes skimpier. It wasn't for the Sunday-school folks."

The burlesque shows, at least in the '50s and '60s, included a lot of old vaudeville stars such as Sally Rand. And Harlem Nights produced at least one later star.

"We were playing in Peoria, Illinois, and this skinny local kid joined Nate's show," Donny recalls. "He cracked up everybody in the cookhouse and around the lot. It got so all the workers were going to the cookhouse if they knew he was there. It was Richard Pryor."

When Donny was 24, he was put in charge of his own carnival. "It was called the World of Pleasure, and I was the absolute, living-end boss. I was elected to the board of directors of the Outdoor Amusement Business Association and put on the committee that ran the conventions."

It was in that capacity that he had an encounter with Colonel Tom Parker, the ex-carny and notoriously hard-nosed manager of Elvis Presley.

"For one of the Las Vegas conventions, he sent me a box of Elvis cards with instructions to set one out at each place at the big dinner. Well, some of the other acts objected, and it made sense not to favor one over another, so I sent them back.

"Then I got a call that he wanted to see me. When I walked into his room I reminded him that we had met when I was a kid, in the office of Sheik Rosen, a Nashville show owner who was a friend of my dad's. He looked me up and down and said, "Yeah, you were a snotty-nosed kid then, and you're a snotty-nosed kid now."

After about a dozen years running carnivals, living in Knoxville during the off-season, Donny settled down, taking over Boblo Island, a large amusement park outside Detroit.

These days he's back in Knoxville, retired and working on a novel based on his Midway experiences.

~~~~~~~~~~

THOUGH I SAW the carny work as my debut in show biz, a previous seasonal job had given me some experience in the limelight. When I was a high school freshman, I had played Santa Claus during a two-week gig in Burlington. Santa was to divide his time between the five and dime and the grocery store across the street. Both were locally owned, the proprietors familiar to me as fellow members of McCalla Avenue Baptist Church.

The Santa suit was property of the five and dime owner, who I'll call Mr. Cash. I was to be paid $1 an hour and would start at 4 p.m. and work until about the 9 p.m. closing time.

I would alternate time in the two stores, though the five and dime soon began to dominate simply because kids tended to linger among the toys there. Mr. Cash, not surprisingly, would encourage me to delay crossing the street to the grocery.

Mr. Cash, notorious in the neighborhood for his strictly business, tight-fisted attitude, didn't like to see me idle. So, when there were no kids in the store, I became the area's only Santa Claus shelf-stocker. When Mr. Wright, the grocer, was told, he had words with Mr. Cash, and I found myself spending more time across the street – there are always customers in a grocery. Even at age 14, I could appreciate the irony of such a conflict during the "Peace on Earth" season.

There were "un-seasonal" episodes in the grocery as well. Twice, mothers used Santa as a threatening device to calm down squirming children as they waited in the check-out line. I was expected to glare menacingly through my Santa face at wide-eyed toddlers.

But my biggest problem came from older kids – my friends. A couple of them came into Cash's when I was seated in my Santa chair and started to harass me, one attempting to sit on my knee. Fortunately, Mr. Cash saw what was going on and chased them out.

So they waited outside until it was time for me to move across the street, providing me with a heckling entourage.

Mr. Wright, whose people skills were much better than those of Mr. Cash, offered to outfit them in elves' costumes. They didn't come around after that.

I survived, though I was certainly glad to see Christmas Eve, knowing that my gig was just about up, and that I would soon be paid $60 for my 12 days under the beard. That was more money than I had ever had at one time.

But Mr. Cash had a surprise for me. An hour or so before I was to turn in my Santa suit, he called me into his office and told me that, since I had not been a full-time Santa, that I had spent several hours re-stocking, he could only pay me 75 cents an hour.

Obviously, I was not happy. And I still had an hour to go, an hour of being jolly on demand.

So I took up my seat with my sack full of holiday-colored ribbon candy to hand out. Mr. Cash had emphasized that each child was to get only one piece. But I had been more generous when he wasn't around. Now, I decided, it was time to get into the spirit of the season. The few children who were still out late on Christmas Eve got handfuls.

Finally, with about ten minutes before closing time, a family of five came in. I recognized the children, a boy and girl of about 10 and 8, and a youngster of about 4. They were residents of one of the tar-papered houses on the wrong side of the ridge where I sometimes delivered newspapers.
Mr. Cash was busy in his office, and his wife was running the cash register out of sight of my station. I loaded up the two older children, cautioning them to put the candy in their

pockets – out of sight. But the toddler was shy, peeking around the counter at me, not sure what this bearded character was all about.

Finally, his sister convinced him that I was okay, and he came up to me. I quickly stuffed his pockets full of candy, and told his sister to make sure he didn't bring out the goodies until they were clear of the store. The mother then came to get them.

"Santa's got to start his deliveries," she said. "It's time to go home." When her daughter gave her mother a peek at all the candy they were toting, she looked at me wide-eyed. I winked. She smiled, and the family headed out the door, my turn at playing Santa Claus at an end.

That night, when I told my dad about Mr. Cash's short-changing ways, he decided that he would not set foot in his store again. As far as I know, he kept his word. And, thanks to my mother, the story quickly spread through the church, adding to Mr. Cash's Scrooge reputation.

~~~~~~~~~~

AFTER THE CHRISTMAS gig, I landed a summer job. It, too, required a uniform of sorts – my full Boy Scout uniform part of the time, the Scout shorts augmented by a Camp Pellissippi t-shirt the rest. And it took me away from home for seven weeks, swapping annoying siblings for an unruly collection of teen-age boys, most of them about my age.

Camp Pellissippi was on Norris Lake north of Knoxville. I referred to myself as a camp counselor, but in reality I was one of the camp's two dishwashers.

Though the job did not carry the noble-sounding "counselor" title, it did pay $20 a week – the counselors only got a couple of dollars credit at the camp trading post. Of course, room and board were included.

For the dishwashers, "room" meant a primitive space underneath the mess hall with three cots and no door. It had been dubbed the Country Club by previous residents.

The other dishwasher, Jim, was a camp veteran about my age; his older brother was the mess-hall director. Jim occupied one of the bunks in the Country Club. The third resident was Rick, a counselor friend of his (they were schoolmates at Karns High School).

Later we made room for a fourth, an East High friend of mine who usually went by his surname, Jenks. He was hired when it was decided that we needed a pot-washer since the pots were too large to fit into the industrial dishwasher that Jim and I used.

Occasionally, always in the middle of the night, the Country Club would host a visitor. The first time he showed up, he scared the bejeebers out of me. I was suddenly awakened by something licking my hand. My yell woke up the rest of the occupants. We caught a glimpse of a dog high-tailing it out. The pooch, a beagle-mix, got used to us (and the handouts we started providing) and became a nighttime regular.

The mess hall, perched on top of a ridge overlooking the lake, was the center of camp – it was the only covered space large enough to house all the campers at once. Plus, it was one of the few camp facilities wired for electricity.

So it was there where the bugler blew Reveille at 7 a.m. and Taps at 11 p.m.

The bugler, domiciled nearby in a large tent covering a wooden platform (most everything in camp was U.S. Army surplus) kept his bugle on a shelf in the mess-hall kitchen. And one night, during a break in one of our marathon games of Hearts, someone noticed the bugle's proximity to the freezer.

The next morning as the bugler frantically searched for his instrument, Jenks found it for him – in the freezer. Already behind schedule, he had to blow Reveille immediately. It was a decidedly sloppy version. With warm water, we helped him remove the mouthpiece from his lips. From then on, he slept with his horn.

The Hearts games would usually start after Taps and often continue until 3 or 4 a.m., usually with five or six participants, including the Country Club residents and sometimes others. One regular was Steve, who ran the Trading Post.

Thanks to his important position as source of chocolate bars and soft drinks, Steve was known to all the campers. And, until one of the directors put a stop to it, he demanded respect at meal time, requiring the campers assigned to his dining table to stand until he sat down and to make sure that he was served first.

Another late-night dining-hall visitor was Hugh, one of the waterfront staffers and unofficial Camp Jester.

Hugh was in his third or fourth year working at Pellissippi, and was renowned for his meal-preparation pantomime. He would place himself at the kitchen's prep counter and pretend he was making meatloaf, kneading and shaping an imaginary concoction. He would moo as he assembled the ingredients, then whack the offending part. Or he would "sneeze" into the "mixture," then, after furtively looking around, begin remixing. Or he would accidentally "cut off" one of his fingers and then add it to the mixture.

Another late-night diversion was the food fight, which generally came on the nights when dessert was pudding, the leftovers providing ammo. Jim and I usually dominated because we had access to the industrial spray gun attached to the dishwasher, which had a reach of about 30 feet. It would then be used to clean the pudding off the walls.

The battles would include lots of shouting and name-calling. Since there was no adult supervision after Taps, and since there were no females present, the name-calling involved a lot of cursing, sometimes with creative combinations. "Fart Breath" was popular until one of the directors overheard its use during a meal.

It was an entertaining seven weeks. And I did learn a few things. I now know how to operate a commercial dishwasher.

I enjoyed a period of being adept at Hearts. And I certainly expanded my vocabulary.

The latter skill caused trouble after camp had ended, and I had not yet adjusted to life in mixed company. At Sunday dinner, when my brother was dawdling over the bowl of mashed potatoes, I used a decidedly unappetizing term in an attempt to speed him up.

So I did without, banished to my room for the rest of the day.

~~~~~~~~~~~

AFTER I OBTAINED a driver's license, my opportunities for part-time work moved beyond the seasonal. Assuring the man doing the hiring, I lied about being able to drive a straight-shift vehicle and landed a position with Swan's, one of the three big bakeries in Knoxville. It was only one day a week (Sunday), but it was year-round.

It came about because the father of one of my high school friends was in charge of the deliveries, and finding and keeping the Sunday-only drivers was always a problem. Most people needed more than one day of work, and the pay was minimum-wage, which at the time was $1.25 an hour.

We had to report at 5:30 a.m., not always easy for teens after a late Saturday night. But the money was helpful, and the work was easier than mowing lawns. Plus, early in our tenure, one of us made a discovery that slightly eased the early-arrival discombobulation.

Swan's had a deal with Krispy-Kreme for daily deliveries of the doughnut chain's fruit-filled fried pies, wrapped individually and packaged 12 to a box. Because of the early hour and the close proximity of the bakery, they would still be warm from the oven. We would then deliver them to groceries on our routes.

One Sunday, one of us had the idea to count the fried pies in each box. We quickly discovered that mistakes were often made in packing the boxes – the numbers were frequently off, with most of the mistakes being in our favor with 13 pies instead of a dozen. We could count on there being at least one extra fried pie for each of us.

Our delivery routes frequently changed, but essentially we each had several large grocery stores – A&P was dominant then, though Kroger had recently moved into the Knoxville market. Then there were a few fast-food restaurants that were open on Sunday; we delivered a lot of hamburger and hot dog buns.

And there were the Cas Walker stores. Walker was a local businessman, politician, and broadcast personality. A school dropout at age 14, he built a successful career by playing to the uneducated, railing against what he perceived as the moneyed elite.

He established his first grocery store when he was in his early 20s, and soon built it into a Knoxville chain, eventually expanding into southeastern Kentucky and southwestern Virginia. He began hosting his own hour-long radio show in 1929, featuring country music and his conservative political harangues. Eventually he was elected to Knoxville's city council, where he served for 30 years. In the late 1940s he won election as Knoxville mayor but was soon recalled after a revolt by the other council members.

In 1954, a newspaper photographer captured Walker taking a swing at one of his cohorts at a city council meeting. The picture, after being broadcast nationally by the Associated Press, was published in Life magazine.

Walker successfully moved his radio show to television in the 1950s – he is credited with providing a major boost to the career of the then teen-aged Dolly Parton after her TV appearances.

During my delivery days, I had stops at several Walker stores – often involving prickly encounters with his store managers.

During one period of my tenure, I began my route on University Avenue at a small café a couple of blocks from Knoxville College in a predominantly black neighborhood. There were a half-dozen tables and a counter with stools. The owner, a slender black man, was always friendly, and depending on how busy he was, usually had a joke or two.

And, though I would be coming through his door early on Sunday morning, he always had several customers, drinking coffee and eating breakfast. Once, when I caught him at a quiet time, I made a comment about how much business he did in spite of the early hour.

He laughed and said, "Everybody comes in to find out who got cut on Saturday night." Deciding to play it straight, I chuckled and told him I'd see him next week.

My second stop was the Cas Walker store two blocks away on Western Avenue. There, the manager was usually difficult, holding a rather high opinion of his position as it related to his suppliers.

His favorite way of demonstrating his power was to be absent when I needed him to count the loaves and buns, a task required at all Cas Walker stores. (Cas was going to make sure he was not being charged for bread he didn't get.) Usually I would find him out back smoking a cigarette or joking with the butcher. He would then wave me off with, "Be with you in a minute." After he had counted and I had priced and shelved, we would walk back to the front of the store so he could pay me from one of the cash registers. (At Cas Walker stores we were always paid cash on delivery.)

And, as we trudged up the aisles, me wrestling with the flattened bread boxes I had just emptied, he would invariably hawk and spit on the floor of his grocery store. If I had needed an excuse not to do any of my own shopping at a Cas Walker store, he provided it.

After we had finished our regular routes, usually by about noon, we would return to the bakery for special orders.

The special orders would be primarily to Blue Circle restaurants, a local chain patterned on the Chattanooga-based Krystal. The Blue Circles, which featured drive-in service as well as inside counters, were popular after-church spots – sometimes we would deliver buns to a couple of their more popular outlets twice in one shift.

My next stop after Cas Walker's was in Lonsdale at Gilbert's Grocery, on Mississippi Avenue, which held the distinction of being my most reliable customer.

Mr. Gilbert, who operated out of what had obviously been built as a small residential dwelling, always wanted the same order: one standard loaf of white bread, wholesale priced, as I remember, at 18 cents.

I never asked Mr. Gilbert why he needed that one loaf of bread on Sundays, but I always suspected that it was for his family dinner. I never saw a customer in his store, though sometimes his wife would be present.

After Gilbert's, I had one more stop before crossing over the interstate into the friendlier environs of Happy Hollow. The Beaumont Milk Depot was a generally cheerful place, operated by a woman who sold staples such as bread, milk, and eggs, but whose primary money-maker was short-orders – hamburgers and hot dogs and soft drinks.

She had a couple of tables and a counter with a few stools, and usually by the late-morning hour when I arrived she had three or four customers, including a friend or two who had stopped by to visit. Sometimes I would pony up for a 50-cent hamburger and eat lunch with her.

One spring morning, just as I was getting ready to leave the store, a car stopped in front, and a shirtless man who looked to be in his late 20s got out of the back passenger side. The driver quickly sped off, with the former passenger angrily yelling at him.

He then turned toward the Depot. Beside my truck, there was a dark blue Chevrolet sitting near the door. Its driver, a female friend of the store's owner, was inside. There was one other customer, a man about 35, also a friend of the owner. Everyone was looking out the open door at Shirtless, who now started yelling at us.

"What are you all looking at?" he wanted to know. He punctuated his question by hitting the trunk of the Chevy with his fist.

"Don't hit my car," the driver said.

Shirtless glared at her, then noticed a lead pipe on the ground at the corner of the building. Arming himself with the pipe, he started hitting the Chevy. Meanwhile, the Depot's owner was calling the police.

The car's owner was screaming and yelling as Shirtless started using the pipe on the car windows, breaking the back windshield, then the front. He moved on to walloping the top, the trunk lid, the hood.

The male customer grabbed a butcher knife from behind the counter and started toward the door, but the rest of us prevented him from going outside.

Finally a couple of police cruisers arrived. Shirtless took one look, then threw the pipe on the ground and stood quietly, waiting to be cuffed.

After explaining to us that Shirtless was "a tush-hog who had been jailed many times," the cop took our eye-witness accounts. Then, as the Chevy's driver was tearfully telling her husband what had happened to their car, I got in my truck and headed to Happy Hollow, where, hopefully, my next stop would be routine.

~~~~~~~~~~

WE NEVER TOLD Mr. Terry, our boss at Swan's, but one Sunday half of his crew – me, Ralph and LaMarr – barely made it to the bakery on time after spending much of Saturday night in the Sevier County jail.

It was a couple of days from Halloween, and we had heard about a haunted house out in the country near Sevierville, in the foothills of the Smoky Mountains about 35 miles from Knoxville. After Ralph got use of his dad's car, and with nothing better to do, we drove up to check it out.

We found the house, standing stark and scary against the night sky on a hilltop. But as we were exiting our car, another vehicle drove up – driven by a Sevier County sheriff's deputy. He was accompanied by a constable. And they wanted to know what we were doing.

Their attitude was sort of casual, and we hadn't done anything wrong, though we were preparing to trespass when they interrupted us. So we weren't particularly frightened, figuring there was no way they could lock us up.

They did frisk us, drawing a chuckle when the constable told me to open up my jacket. "You might have a machine gun under there," he said with a grin.

Of course, our story about a haunted house wasn't exactly believable. So they decided to take us back to the jail, ordering us into the back seat of the police car. Our protests were led by Ralph, the pragmatic member of the trio – he did not want to leave his dad's black, four-door '53 Chevrolet. Later we accused him of being worried more about losing his prize Baby Moon hubcaps than he was of his dad's car disappearing in rural Sevier County in the dark of night.

Finally, a compromise was reached. LaMarr and I would ride in the cruiser, the constable would accompany Ralph, following us in the Chevy.

At the courthouse in downtown Sevierville – the jail was in the rear – we were questioned one at a time in a separate room. The first one to be questioned was Ralph, who told us when he returned that the case had something to do with stolen tobacco.

It turned out that the deputy was looking for a crew of teen-agers who had broken into a farmer's barn to steal his burley. The farmer had caught them, but one of them had pulled a knife, and they had escaped.

The farmer was brought in to look us over, one by one. There was already a problem with the deputy's case – there were four of the thieves, and they had been in a blue and white '55 Ford. Of course, the farmer didn't recognize any of us. So after an hour of so, we were released – with a warning to stay away from the haunted house.

The warning was unnecessary; we had already decided to get out of Sevier County as soon as possible. On the trip back to

Knoxville, there was a lot of talk built around boasts that if the farmer had identified us, "We would eventually have had his tobacco, his barn and his whole farm."

After our close call, we made it to Swan's, happy for once to be wide-awake and reporting for duty at 5:30 a.m.

~~~~~~~~~~

BY THE TIME of that escapade, my friends and I were veterans of late-night rides around Knoxville. One of us – I'll call him Slick here – was already a legend among the car-crazed at East High. He had obtained his own ride while the rest of us were still stuck with the family automobile. True, his car was a Henry J, squat, sort of toad-like in appearance, with an anemic power plant. But it was actually Slick's, not his parents', and that put him way ahead of the rest of us. We had to "Yes sir" and "No ma'am" around the house all week long for a shot at the family station wagon on Saturday night.

Slick had big plans for the Henry J – but within weeks he had rolled it. The car was totaled, but Slick walked away relatively unscathed. And this was in the 1960s, before seatbelts came into general use.

The wreck and Slick's survival only cemented his reputation at East. He was already known in our circle as a fearless and fast driver. When I would ask my mother if I could use the station wagon, Slick's name usually came up, as in "You're not going to do something stupid like Slick, are you?"

So now, the Henry J in a junkyard, Slick was quick to express his admiration when Gary Killian bought a '51 Ford, black with three-on-the-column. Sure, the upholstery was ragged, and the front driver's side sported a snow tire, making handling a bit tricky. But, Slick pointed out, the back seat looked like it had never been used, and there was a flathead V8 under the hood.

Besides, he said, a '49, '50, or '51 Ford was the best possible car to own in East Tennessee. He argued that no matter where you might break down, you were no more than 200 yards from one up on blocks. That meant that parts would never be a problem.

Not long after he bought the Ford, Killian decided to accompany his parents to Florida for a week's vacation. He rashly left the keys with Slick.

Killian departed on a Sunday, and on Sunday night Slick was out front of my house in the Ford. He was accompanied by his next-door neighbor, Carl, and another friend who went by the nickname of Bear.

"There's a swingin' A&W Root Beer down in Madisonville," Slick said by way of explanation. Madisonville was about 50 miles south of Knoxville. I got in.

Our first stop was just outside of town, at the bridge across the Tennessee River. We stopped for a hitchhiker. In the early '60s, it was still relatively common, and safe, to thumb rides. Our hitcher was a soldier in uniform, carrying a duffel bag.

"Where you all headed?" he asked as he climbed into the back with Carl and Bear, settling the duffel between his legs.

"Don't know," said Bear.

"Where you headed?" asked Slick, turning his head from the driver's position. Even though it was night and pitch dark, Slick was wearing mirrored sunglasses, the kind that the comedian Brother Dave Gardner favored. Slick patterned himself after Brother Dave, even to the Southern-preacher pompadour.

"Fort Benning," said the soldier.

"That's in Georgia," said Carl, real matter of fact.

"Well, we might just take you all the way to Fort Benning," said Slick.

"Yeah," said Bear. "I never been to Georgia."

"Yeah, maybe we ought to just take you all the way to Fort Benning," said Slick, easing back onto the highway.

"It don't matter to us," said Bear. "Car's not ours anyway, so we might as well take you to Georgia."

The soldier laughed, but he looked uncomfortable.

"Awwww, man," said Slick, warming to his new audience. "Georgia would probably be a good place to go. Is there a beach near there?"

No, Benning's nowhere near a beach, the soldier explained.

"If we can drive to Georgia," said Carl, "we can drive to the beach."

"Car's not ours anyway," said Bear.

The soldier was looking real uncomfortable, probably seeing himself party to a gang of car thieves, crossing state lines, breaking innumerable laws both civilian and military.

By now we were on the other side of Maryville, and, Slick announced, running low on gas. The soldier, seeing the possibility for escape, started to look relieved.

Here commenced our regular argument. Carl and Bear claimed they had no money. I joined them. Our hitchhiker didn't say anything.

"Awwww, man," said Slick, "we go through this every time. I'm the one got the car; I'm the one doing the driving. No reasonable person's going to expect me to pay for the gas, too."

Finally, Carl owned up to a dollar – three and a half gallons of regular. Slick pulled into the next station, where the soldier grabbed his duffel and jumped out. "Thanks," he said, "but I'll see if I can catch a ride with somebody more sure about where they're going."

Slick was jawing with the gas jockey when a kid looked like he was about 14 walked up. You all going south? he asked Carl.

"Madisonville, the A&W," Carl answered. "Need a ride?"

"Yeh," said the kid. "I'm going to Etowah."

"Well," said Bear, "we can get you as far as Madisonville. Not our car, so it makes no difference to us."

The kid climbed into the seat vacated by the soldier. Slick handed over Carl's dollar, and, just for show, threw a little gravel as he gunned it out onto Highway 411.

In less than a mile, our headlights caught a small white cross beside the highway. What was that, Bear asked.

"This road's known as Bloody 411," Carl said, "because of all the people who have been killed pulling out just like we did back there. The Rotary or somebody puts up those white crosses every place somebody gets killed."

"Just as a reminder to people like us," Slick said with a smirk.

"You ever hang out at the Madisonville A&W," I asked the kid. "We hear it's a swinging place."

"Some," said the kid. "Used to go there before I left Etowah."

"When did you leave Etowah?" asked Carl.

"This morning," said the kid. "Ran away from home after I broke up with my girl."

"Most people run away from home, they take some clothes and stuff, don't they?" asked Carl.

"Yeah, I guess," said the kid. "That's one reason I decided to go back once I got to Maryville."

"Girls make you do some funny things," said Bear.

"I reckon," said the kid.

Suddenly, the car started wobbling.

"Awwww, man," said Slick. "What's the matter now?"

"Sounds like a flat tire," said the kid, glad to change the subject.

We pulled into the next service station. The front passenger-side tire was flat. In the trunk, we found a spare – another snow tire – but no jack. The man running the station, not too friendly, said we couldn't use his, but three guys hanging around a '56 Chevy loaned us theirs.

"Where's your all's jack?" asked the kid.

"Don't know," said Bear. "Not our car."

"Oh," said the kid. He didn't seem too concerned about the car's ownership.

"There should be a lot less highway hum now we got snow tires on both sides upfront," said Slick. "Make this baby easier to steer, too."

"A&W'll be on the left," said the kid as we neared Madisonville. "I'll probably be able to find a ride on to Etowah there."

"Better circle this place a couple of times before we park," said Slick as we pulled into the A&W. "So they'll know we're here."

We found a good spot, under the awning out on the end, and backed in. Slick revved the flathead before shutting it down.

The kid saw a friend in an old Plymouth and climbed out. "Much obliged," he said.

"Yeah," said Slick. "Don't take any wooden nickels."

Bear had his head out the window, perusing the menu. "I don't reckon I've ever had a root beer," he said.

"And I don't reckon you remember 30 minutes ago when we were buying gas and you said you had no money whatsoever, either, do you?" said Slick.

"Oh, yeah," said Bear. "I don't have any money."

Slick ordered a root beer and Carl got a footlong hot dog. I kept my eyes peeled for any swingin' action.

"All the girls seem to be with some hairyleg," observed Bear.

"Yeah," added Slick, " I don't see much in the way of opportunity."

"Might help," said Carl, "if you'd take off those sunglasses."

Slick ignored him and slowly finished his root beer. Finally, after a last slurp, he put the cup on the tray and flashed the lights for the carhop. "What say we blow this joint," he said. "Sunday must not be the night in Madisonville."

The flathead roared into action, and Slick threw a gravel roostertail a good 10 yards long. We waved to the kid, now talking to some girl, and hit the highway back toward Knoxville.

About a dozen miles down the highway, three-quarters up a long, curving hill, the flathead sputtered to a stop.

"Awwww, man, we're out of gas again," said Slick. He let the car roll backwards and onto the shoulder. Nothing, not even a light, in either direction. Only thing in sight was a trio of white crosses right where we were stopped. Slick got out and tried to wave down the first car that passed. No luck.

Then, headed in the opposite direction, came the fellows who had loaned us the jack.

"What's the matter?" asked the driver. "Another flat tire?"

"Out of gas," said Slick.

They volunteered a ride back to the service station, and the usual argument over money commenced, with Bear keeping his mouth shut. Finally, I owned up to a dollar, and Slick pitched in another. Then he climbed into the Chevy and they roared off.

Ten minutes later, after we had watched a few semis speed by, the Chevy returned, the driver executing a righteous four-wheel slide in the middle of the highway. Slick climbed out, two-gallon gas can in his hand.

"Much obliged," he yelled as the Chevy sped off toward Madisonville.

Slick poured gas into the Ford.

"Better keep some back to prime the carburetor," said Carl. "Specially since we're sitting nose up a hill."

"Awwww, man," said Slick. "I don't need you to tell me what to do. I've done this a few times."

"Bet you have," said Carl.

With the hood raised, Carl behind the wheel, me and Bear standing outside watching, Slick primed the carburetor. Carl turned the ignition, but the Ford wouldn't start.

"Kick it off," said Slick. "Put it into reverse and roll it down the highway backwards and kick it off."

Carl slipped it into reverse, pushed in the clutch and rolled back out onto the highway. The hood was still up. Then, down at the bottom of the hill, coming around the curve, was a semi, building up speed to climb the grade. Instead of trying to kick it off, Carl started grinding the ignition.

"Pop the clutch, you ignorant sumbitch," yelled Slick.

Finally, the semi's driver laying on his airhorn, Carl popped the clutch and the flathead roared to life. Carl shifted into first and came flying up the highway weaving side-to-side, because the hood was still up and he couldn't see where he was going.

We were yelling at him, and then he was coming straight at us, head out the window trying to see. As we scattered through the crosses, the semi, doing at least 70, pulled into the southbound lane and roared around the Ford. Carl, the car now mostly on the shoulder, stopped.

"Don't shut it off," said Slick.

Carl pulled on the handbrake and climbed out. "That was close," he said.

"I would think," said Slick, now behind the wheel, "that you would need to wring out your underwear after that ride."

The rest of us took up our positions. We dropped the gas can off at the service station, spending the rest of the $2 on five gallons of regular. There wasn't much said on the ride back. We didn't see any more hitchhikers. About the time we got close to my house, the flathead started sputtering.

"Awwww, man," said Slick. "Not again."

He coasted into the Love's Creek gas station, and the money argument started. I slipped out and walked on home.

Working

*Blue notes, roadhouses, and bandstands – Faces
of tragedy – Bank robbers and burgers –
Tondalaya and the long-legged June Knight –
Stakeouts and close calls in the private-dick trade*

~~~~~~~~~~

THOUGH I NEVER learned to play any instrument, I always
had an interest in music, catching "Your Hit Parade" on
television by the time I was 6 or 7 years old. The 1950s' show
featured the popular songs of the time performed by various
singers, one of whom sported the memorable name of
Snooky Lanson. Another was a cute, sexy brunette named
June Valli.

Though the show featured the often-boring songs of the time,
the production values were high, with excellent
musicianship.

Then rock 'n' roll came along, and through that, I discovered
its antecedent, blues. And a kid named Vance Walker showed
up at East High School, having moved with his family from
Alabama.

Vance was a self-taught guitarist, and his primary
inspirations were Jimmy Reed, Bobby "Blue" Bland, and
Bukka White. Soon, I was a serious blues fan, and that led me
to jazz.

The first record I bought was a 45, "Sack of Woe" by Cannonball Adderley. I confess that I selected it primarily because of Mr. Adderley's cool nickname.

Vance favored blues and rock 'n' roll, but he taught himself to play by listening to Chet Atkins records; by the time he graduated high school he was proficient in a lot of genres.

At an East High School Talent Day gathering when he was a junior, Vance joined three senior musicians on the auditorium stage. Their music had most of the student body rocking in their seats as nervous teachers and administrators squirmed. Finally, at the performance climax, an extended riff on Jimmy Reed's blues standard, "Baby, What You Want Me to Do?" one of the teachers went backstage and turned off the power. A near riot was averted by stern looks from principal Buford Bible, who had taken over the microphone.

But one unplugging didn't deter Vance. He moved on to playing lead for popular local singer Clifford Russell and jamming with his older cousin, a keyboardist who was an in-demand fixture of the East Tennessee roadhouse scene, adept whether the occasion called for country, rock 'n' roll, blues or gospel.

Vance and his cousin led to my one gig as a roadie. One Saturday morning, sometime in 1967, Vance called – he was seeking someone to help out with a last-minute job that night. The opportunity had begun an hour or so earlier with a panic-induced call to Vance's cousin.
They would be playing at the Indian Rock Grill, Vance told me, pointing out that Jerry Lee Lewis had performed there.

The Indian Rock was in east Knox County on Rutledge Pike, a roadhouse that was frequently in the news for all the wrong reasons, infamous for fights and arrests and violations of liquor laws. Jerry Lee Lewis, his career then in a tailspin due to backlash because of marriage to his 13-year-old cousin, had performed there a couple of times – that was as close as the place got to positive press.

Vance's cousin had received a call from the Indian Rock's owner – the regular band had cancelled. A quartet was quickly assembled, with Vance on guitar and vocals. The group would play for the door. I got the nod because they needed someone to collect the cover charge.

Of course, I saw the call as an opportunity to be associated with rising rock 'n' rollers, with a famous venue and, by a dubious stretch, with Jerry Lee Lewis. "What time do I show up for the gig?" I asked, employing a term that I was sure made me appear to be a seasoned veteran of the music scene.

I helped the four unload their equipment (amplifiers, a drum set, and most notably because of its weight and unwieldy size, a Hammond B3 organ with Leslie tone cabinet). After the stage was set up, I pulled a stool to the door and counted the bills I had brought along for making change. The cover charge, it was decided, would be $2.

There was time for the band to run through a couple of songs before the first customers – two women – showed up. They listened for a bit, asked me where the regular band was, and then wanted to know who the group on stage was. I told them they didn't have a name yet. They listened for a couple more minutes, looked at each other, said something about checking out the Oak Grove, and left. The Oak Grove, which was nearby on Asheville Highway, boasted the same kind of reputation as the Indian Rock.

The pair's reaction, unfortunately, was a harbinger of the evening. After a couple more departures, I began distancing myself from the band, telling would-be customers that I didn't know who they were, only that they were a last-minute substitute. I would point out that the cover was only $2.

A handful of revelers paid up and found tables. There was some dancing. Vance and the others began making their jams longer and longer as they ran out of tunes that all four were familiar with. I was adding, "They don't sound too bad on some songs" to my banter with would-be customers.

At closing time, the take totaled $22. After we had managed to get the Hammond and other equipment loaded back up, we split the money. The band members got $5 each and I was given the remaining $2. Vance and I then took our money and went to the Oak Grove, where the crowd was enjoying a classic roadhouse mix of country and rock 'n' roll by the joint's regular band. The woman on the door knew Vance and generously let us in without charge, leaving us with just enough money for a good time.

~~~~~~~~~~

AFTER MY FRESHMAN year at East High, my parents decided to lease our house in Burlington and move to Maryville so Dad could be closer to his job at the Alcoa plant.

So we moved to a house on Everett High Road, just one door away from the Everett school complex. The complex included four or five buildings and grades 1 through 12, which meant that my sister and brother and I could all walk to school since the schools were in the same location.

My siblings, who would have been in the seventh and third grades, were unhappy about the move, but I don't recall thinking much about it one way or the other. Maybe I was still upset about not getting to move to Trinidad a few years earlier.

I quickly made friends with a couple of guys who were old enough to drive. And one of them frequently had access to his brother's car. My dad had given me his golf clubs, which consisted of a spoon (three-wood), a mashie (five-iron), and a putter, all in a small golf bag. "Those three clubs are all you really need," he explained. He was speaking from experience – in his teen years, he had caddied at the Holston Hills Country Club course. Lugging heavy bags full of clubs for 18 holes might have influenced his outlook on the number of clubs actually necessary.

So my new friends and I took my three clubs to the front lawn of the Maryville College campus, where there were a couple of unkempt holes. We practiced, sure that we were getting better.

Finally, after saving our money for several weeks, one Saturday we played the nine-hole course at Wallace Hills, south of town. Determined to get our money's worth, we played 31 holes, finally quitting when it got too dark to see the flags. Seeing the balls didn't matter as much, because we rarely hit them squarely anyway.

Another Everett acquaintance was Jerry LeQuire. He was a year older and was in one of my classes – we didn't pal around, but years later I was reminded that I had known him when he made the news. He distinguished himself with audacious criminal activity, smuggling drugs from South America into the U.S. Reportedly, he hid more than $300 million in profits. He died in prison in 2014, the money, if it existed, never located.

I encountered another Everett friend under tragic circumstances when I started working at the Journal in my sophomore year at the University of Tennessee. The newspaper had a policy of publishing a photograph of victims of automobile accidents, and one of my duties as a copy boy was to pick up the picture from the victim's family. One of the reporters would make the arrangements, and then I would take a staff car to the home.

One night, handed the address of a Blount County victim, I saw a familiar name. It was a classmate whom I knew well from school and from church. I picked up the photograph from one of his siblings and told him that I knew his brother in high school. It was a tough experience.

A few weeks later, I stood on the north Knoxville front porch of a young suicide victim whom I also knew, through his

Golden Gloves boxing. His mother handed me his picture while his widow, holding their infant, sobbed quietly. I nervously expressed my sorrow and told them that I knew him, that I had seen him fight several times. "He loved boxing," his widow said. "He just loved boxing."

Picking up the photographs was one of the more serious of my copy-boy duties. Most were routine – keeping reporters and editors fueled with caffeine paramount. During an eight-hour shift, I might make a dozen trips to the nearby Blue Circle or Krystal for coffee, adding hamburgers and French fries during the dinner hour.

~~~~~~~~~~

WHEN I STARTED at the Journal, one of the old hands had given me a tour of the facilities. One stop was the newspaper's library, known in the business as the "morgue." There, I was introduced to Clarence Bunch. In Bunch's case, the "morgue" nickname was appropriate.

Vic Weals, one of the Journal's longtime staffers, was my guide, and he played the tour for all it was worth. He showed me the long, narrow room, consisting of a central aisle flanked by rows of file cabinets. He stopped at a couple of the cabinets, pulling out files with photos of Marilyn Monroe and Ava Gardner. Then there was a drawer with decks of playing cards behind the files. "These belong to Bob Adams, the wire editor," Vic explained. "He keeps them stashed in here and plays solitaire late at night. But that's not all he stashes."

And he opened another drawer and showed me a bag of in-the-shell peanuts. "He likes his peanuts, too."

Later, I learned that Stealing Bob's Peanuts was a popular game among the staff. And there was the time when, after Adams, who had a tendency toward arrogance, provoked several staffers before going home for the night. His decks of cards were assembled and one card taken from each before they were put back into their hiding places. I don't think he ever figured out why he couldn't win.

After the hiding places were revealed, Vic went to the far end of the room where there were a couple of desks for the librarians. Behind the desks was a cabinet with slim, deep drawers designed to hold full-page broadsheet newspapers.

In one of those drawers was a copy of the Journal's front page from August 22, 1934. The lead story was of Clarence Bunch's death during a police shootout at a house in Park City, a couple of miles east of downtown. As he stepped out onto the front porch of the house, he was accompanied by the Grainger County sheriff and a deputy, mysteriously several miles outside their jurisdiction.

When confronted by the Knoxville police gathered in front of him, Bunch grabbed the Grainger sheriff's pistol and opened fire. The outlaw was then hit by about two dozen bullets (one news account says 23, another 26). The Grainger sheriff and deputy were later charged with harboring a fugitive.

So that there could be no doubt that Bunch was dead, the story included a six-column picture of the corpse lying on a slab in the county morgue, dried blood caked around the entry wounds. It was that image that Vic wanted to show me.

The resumé of Bunch, a contemporary of other widely known Depression-era outlaws, included armed robbery and jail escape. He had fled the Cocke County jail in Newport in July and had been on the lam for about a month. Given his law-enforcement companions on the porch, he obviously possessed charm and leadership ability.

Bunch's body, embalmed and on display at a downtown funeral home, drew crowds of the curious – hundreds, the newspapers reported.

Later, when I told my dad about viewing the front page, while we were eating lunch at a popular Burlington café, he laconically informed me that he was familiar with Bunch. Pressed, he said that our host at the eatery, who was an acquaintance, had gotten into the restaurant business because of Bunch.

After his escape from the Cocke County jail, Bunch and his gang (two others had escaped with him) had terrorized motorists in East Tennessee. A favorite ploy was to pull up behind a traveler and shoot out the tires, forcing the driver to stop. Then the driver and occupants would be robbed. Reportedly, sometimes the ensuing roadblock would lead to other victims, causing "robbery jams" on Asheville Highway and Rutledge Pike and other country thoroughfares.

Sometime in late July, my dad said, Knoxville police got word that Bunch was heading into Knoxville on Asheville Highway, which became Magnolia Avenue at Burlington. A roadblock was set up.

Sure enough, Bunch and his boys were spotted. But they blasted their way through the roadblock and were pursued down Magnolia, guns blazing. In the melee, two of the policemen, both friends of my dad's, were close behind Bunch, close enough that a bullet hit their windshield, scattering glass. The passenger was cut by flying glass.

"Bleeding, he thought he had been hit by a bullet and made his partner stop the car," Dad said. "He got out and then and there quit the force. It turned out to be a cut from the glass, easily taken care of with a few stitches. But he didn't go back to the force.

"He decided to open a restaurant instead."

So the sandwiches that we just ate came about because of a notorious outlaw?

"You can thank Clarence Bunch for your hamburger and fries," Dad said.

~~~~~~~~~~~

I HAD BEEN WORKING at the Journal for a couple of days when I met Grady Amann, of the sports department. He would become one of my best friends as well as my guide to the ins and outs of the newspaper trade.

My introduction to Grady came one afternoon as I was performing a key task, picking up photos to take to the engraving department. The basket was on a cabinet next to Grady's desk. This was when copy was typed onto double pages of paper separated by carbon paper. Stray sheets of carbon paper were common – and slippery.

When I went butt-up after stepping on one in front of Grady's desk, he jumped to his feet, pointed at me and said, "Hey, no dancing!" I had to laugh in spite of my embarrassment.

A couple of weeks later, I saw a familiar face getting off the elevator one afternoon. Mr. Bradley, my fairgrounds employer, stepped into the office and spotted me.

"Where have you been?" he said as greeting. "I've been looking for you to work the duck pond when we open."

I explained that I had a new, more permanent job. He was in the Journal seeking publicity, so I directed him to the city desk. He waved as he left, and I realized that my carny career was at an end. But, of course, I would be sneaking into the fair during its run.

A few days later I ran into an old high school buddy and another fairgrounds veteran. I'll call him Dickson. The same year that I took up my zoo popcorn stand position, he began work as a uniformed attendant of the inside-the-grounds parking lots. His employer was a well-known security outfit, which meant he got to wear an official-looking uniform.

On anyone else, the spiffy, crisp outfit might have looked impressive. But on Dickson, who resembled Woody Allen, it looked comical. Blue pants with white stripes down the outside edge of each leg, white shirt with blue company logo. A blue cop hat with shiny black brim topped off the ensemble, almost overwhelming Dickson's horn-rimmed glasses. When he showed up at the zoo the day of the fair's opening, I had to laugh. He just grinned.

"You won't laugh when you hear where I've been assigned," he said. Though he might have looked like a cartoon version of a cop, he was full of confidence – in fact, most times Dickson could not be headed no matter how stupid his scheme of the moment. And Dickson was a schemer.

True, my stand at the zoo was about as low as a fair job could get, across the walkway from the animals – two aged lions and a battery of monkeys. But at 7 p.m. I would close up and move to Bradley's duck pond.

Dickson usually had a job directing cars. Somehow, he had talked his way into a promotion, and here he was, outfitted seriously, armed with a new flashlight, one of those double-long, four-battery truncheons.

"While you're playing straight man to a cage full of monkeys," he said, "starting in a half hour, I'm working behind the girly show on the Midway, making sure no one sneaks in by climbing the fence behind the tent."

He put a lot of emphasis on that last clause, because we were all familiar with that particular stretch of fence. Before we had gone legit with real jobs at the fair, before we had taken to calling ourselves "carnies," we had become adept at sneaking into the fairgrounds. The fence behind the girly show had been a favorite – it was dark and off the main roads – until a couple of years earlier when the Midway operators had stationed a guard there. And now Dickson was telling me that he was that guard.

So that first night, about 10 p.m. I drifted away from the duck pond and made my way to Dickson's spot. When the girls were changing costumes, we could almost see more than was possible with a paid ticket and a front-row seat. There was just enough promise to induce neck-stretching and quiet re-positioning.

Of course, when we explained to our friends, we exaggerated, and by the second night we were being joined by three or four others, all of us hunkered down behind the tent. We especially lusted after the long-legged June Knight, the show's star, and Tondelaya, who was spectacularly configured.

 So we spent each night of the fair's run in goggle-eyed effort at cheap thrills. But the fair only ran for 10 days, and June Knight and Tondelaya were soon on to their next stop. We returned to our weekend-night routine of cruising the drive-ins, the girly show replaced by awkward efforts at conversation with the girls in the cars next to us at the Pizza Palace or the Tic-Toc.

Then, a couple of weeks after the fair, I got a call from Dickson. He had an assignment, he said, and he wanted to know if I could drive. An assignment?

Yeah, he said, for the security outfit. He was, he informed me, still doing work for them, important work, private-detective work. "You are talking to a full-fledged private dick," he said. He wanted me to drive, because, he added, he didn't think his Volkswagen bug was quick enough.

I was driving a 1960 3.4 Litre Jaguar sedan, a giant leap from my previous wheels, the family station wagon. I was the envy of my group, though Vance Walker insisted that his dad's pink and white 1957 Cadillac was faster and cooler.

But I had an advantage – the Jag was mine, bought with money I made from my full-time job as a cub reporter. I needed no one's permission to take it out. And because of my regular employment, I always had gas money.

I didn't take a lot of convincing, and agreed to pick up Dickson in front of his house about 8:30 p.m. on Saturday. He would, he confided mysteriously, fill me in on the way to Maryville. As usual, his mother followed him out the sidewalk, telling him to be careful and to be home early. And, as usual, he acted like she wasn't even there.

As it turned out, we were headed through Maryville, to a service station south of town on U.S. 129. There we were to meet the client, a woman who was trying to gather evidence on her cheating husband.

The woman was accompanied by her sister. They told us to park our car and ride with them. On the short trip Dickson tried to impress the women. "Your husband said anything suspicious?" he wanted to know. "Made any rash moves, done anything stupid?" He mentioned the name Marilee, explaining to me that she was the "other woman."

"And she's not even good-looking," the wronged wife added with a sniff as we pulled into the driveway of a brick rancher. Dickson and I quietly crept around back to the basement entry while the two women made their way through the house so they could open the sliding-glass doors into the basement recreation room.

Dickson had tapped the client's phone and set up a tape recorder on top of an air-conditioning duct. He needed to change the tape, he said. Fifteen minutes at most, he added.

Just as he was climbing up to reach the recorder, there was a noise upstairs. We froze. The client decided to go see what was going on. Dickson and I, without conferring, decided to go out the sliding-glass door into the woods behind the house. Soon, the woman's sister rounded us up. False alarm, she said – the cat had knocked over his food dish.

We went back, Dickson changed the tape, and we soon hit the highway for Knoxville. So how do you like being a private eye, Dickson wanted to know. Not much to it, I said – as long as the husband doesn't show up. Dickson just laughed. "These guys aren't very smart," he said, smug in his private-eye persona. "You should hear some of the stupid things he says on the phone when he's talking to his girlfriend. When he's not being all smoochy, he's laughing about his wife not knowing anything."

My next "assignment" was a stake-out, keeping Dickson company while we sat in his car across the highway from the client's house. I had convinced him that his VW was less conspicuous than my Jag. I soon found that all the assignments were installing phone taps, changing the tapes, or fidgeting inconspicuously through stakeouts.

The work was steady, and Dickson soon had enough money for a more suitable vehicle. He found a Jag similar to mine, and, in his arrogance, ignored my observation about it being easy to spot. "The people we're dealing with," he said, "they don't know a Jaguar from a '49 Plymouth."

Perhaps inevitably, there was a close call during a daytime assignment where he was changing a tape in a basement garage. I was working at my own job, and therefore wasn't along. The suspected adulterer returned home unexpectedly, and Dickson had to stay hidden behind the furnace for more than an hour before he could get out. After listening to his tale, told with the braggadocio that only comes after the fact, I decided to get out of the private-dick business, refusing any more "assignments."

Next time I saw Dickson, he was involved in one of Knoxville's most high-profile divorce cases, a mess that I knew a lot about because of late-night newsroom talk with the reporters.

The battle was over child custody. The husband, a prominent doctor, was seeking to have his wife declared an unfit mother. She was, according to courthouse scuttlebutt and testimony, sex-crazed. She liked to sun herself nude in their fenced backyard, testimony revealed. She had been known to answer the door without clothes.

And, most damning, the maid testified that she had applied ointment to madam's rug burns, suffered during sex on the floor with a well-known actor who was in Knoxville for the making of a movie.

At first Dickson's job was tapping the phone for the husband. But by that time, the ex-wife was coy enough not to reveal anything over the phone lines. The husband and his lawyer decided more drastic measures were needed.

So Dickson and one of our high school buddies, Randall, came up with a plan. Randall's parents moved in the same circles as the doctor and his wife; he had met the woman a couple of times.

And he had a decent apartment off-campus. He would, he announced, lure her to his place for an assignation. A photographer would then burst in through the unlocked door and, flashbulbs popping, catch the couple in a compromising position.

Dickson wanted me to be the photographer. "Money up front," he said. "And it's the kind of job that could lead to something big. If this works, the three of us could open our own agency, specializing in high-profile cases just like this one."

I declined. "Okay," he said, "but you'll be sorry after we start working on all kinds of juicy capers. We'll be like Mike Mannix and you'll be writing stories about us." The reference was to a popular television detective.

"Stories about you all being shot," I answered.

I finally agreed to loan them a camera and show Dickson how to use it. Dickson and Randall then ran through a few practice bust-ins at Randall's apartment. I stayed away, though I did develop their efforts in the newspaper's darkroom.

After a couple of rolls of film, Dickson finally figured out how to focus the camera on the bed. But then he made a mistake. He left the pictures on his bedside table, and his mother noticed them.

"What's this all about?" she wanted to know. Dickson's explanations didn't convince her. Eventually, the truth came out. And Dickson's career as a private dick was at an end. Soon, he was telling me about his new job – he was parking cars again, this time at a downtown lot.

"Parked a Corvette the other day," he informed me with a smirk. "Got rubber all the way across the lot."

A Sixties Education

Doc and the Cowboy – Sweet William –
Poolrooms and the Knoxville Bear – Squeegee
and other Strip characters – Moonshine in the
mountains – Up the creek with Jim Dykes –
Playmate of the Year – Lenny and the hooker –
Going to the game with Rod

~~~~~~~~~~~

NOT LONG AFTER I bought the Jaguar, I decided to move out
of my parents' house in east Knox County into the Fort
Sanders area, closer to my UT classes and to my downtown
Journal workplace. I found a place in a dilapidated two-story
building that had initially been built as a motel for folks who
needed a temporary place close to Fort Sanders Hospital, a
half-block away. At some point, students had taken it over.

The building was at 1818 Laurel Avenue, only three blocks
from the Strip, the section of Cumberland Avenue between
17th Street and the railroad overpass six blocks west. The
Strip was the heart of the campus's business district,
dominated by restaurants and bars. On weekend nights, it
was hopping.

Since 1818 was designed as a motel, the building's units
consisted of one small room and a shower-equipped bath. A
bed was included, but no storage cabinets. I talked my

mother into letting me take a chest of drawers, necessary linens and towels and an electric skillet.

The Journal didn't publish on Sunday, so I always had Saturdays off, reporting back to work at 5 p.m Sunday. And since the rest of my friends were still living at home, my room was soon a popular Saturday-night gathering spot, though five was about capacity.

At one of the gatherings, one of my neighbors from upstairs heard the ruckus and came down and introduced himself. He'll be called Roy here. He was an animal-science major, and though the ridges and valleys of East Tennessee are far removed from the cattle-raising plains of the West, he was a true cowboy. A senior in his early 20s, he already was a successful rancher, leasing pasturage in a nearby county for his beef cattle. In his junior year he had sold one-third of a blue-ribbon bull for $10,000, testament to the animal's breeding potential.

Roy exhibited Hollywood-cowboy traits, too. He was taciturn when sober and rowdy when drunk. And he was known to sometimes carry a .38 revolver.

It was because of Roy that I learned about Knoxville's leading abortion doctor. Abortion then was a shadowy, illegal practice. The Doc was a general practitioner whose office hours were 5 p.m. to 9 p.m. three days a week. His office was on the fringe of downtown, less than a mile from our apartments. (Here, he will be called the Doc; the other names have been changed.)

Roy had come to me in an uncharacteristic panic. He had gotten a girl pregnant, and he asked if I knew where she could get an abortion. Roy knew that I had contacts through my job at the Journal. I asked the police reporter, and he gave me the name of the Doc. I passed the information along. I didn't see Roy for a couple of weeks, and I assumed that he and his girlfriend had visited the Doc.

But the Doc's name came up again a few weeks later when my friend Nick came to me with the same problem. His girlfriend Jeannie was pregnant.

Nick and Jeannie were involved in a more stable relationship than Roy was. But when Jeannie's pregnancy had been confirmed, they had decided not to have the baby.

Nick wasn't mature enough for fatherhood and Jeannie was well aware of that. Indeed, a couple of months later, Nick would be making another trip to the Doc's – with another girlfriend.

In 1967, the options available to those confronted with an unwanted pregnancy were limited. The Pill had been available for a few years, but to most it was still a novelty, controversial. Roe v. Wade was five years away.

Knoxville had a home run by the Florence Crittenton agency, a national organization founded in 1896 to provide a discreet place where unwed mothers-to-be could stay during their last three months of pregnancy. But Knoxville girls, at least those with the means, usually opted to spend their pregnancies at Crittenton facilities in Nashville or Memphis, returning after the baby had been born and adopted. That way the pregnancy could be kept quiet, their absence explained as an extended visit with relatives or, in the case of one of my friends, as a lengthy treatment for a mysterious "infection."

 Such visits depended on having the contacts and on being able to take time away from jobs or school.

Another option was the Mexican abortion – Tijuana was popular. But Mexico is a long way from Knoxville, and Jeannie could not afford to miss work.

The Doc provided another option. As I recall, the Doc's fee was $200. For Nick, the trip to the Doc simply meant a month or two of drinking less, catching his executive father in a generous mood with a convincing story or borrowing the money from friends.

Nick cadged the $200 from a fraternity brother and made an appointment. Immediately after the procedure, Jeannie, pale and shaken, rested in my apartment; the Doc had no recovery facilities, and Nick lived in the frat house.

Later, through my job, I became friends with an emergency-room nurse. She knew about the Doc. And she knew about the girls without the knowledge or the means to visit him. Occasionally, she would be involved in the treatment of a girl who had attempted an abortion either alone or with help, often of the coat-hanger variety.

There had not been any recent deaths in Knoxville from such methods, but she had heard stories from veteran co-workers, stories that I did not want to hear. But that all came later, after Roy's situation resulted in a first-hand encounter with a time-tested southern Appalachian solution to unexpected pregnancy.

Whatever Roy and his girlfriend had decided, her family had their own ideas, and one night shortly after Nick's girlfriend had recovered in my apartment, I was awakened by yelling outside my window.

The father of Roy's girlfriend, flanked by his two sons, was facing the building's balcony, where Roy was standing, shirtless, revolver in hand. The girl was behind her dad.

The yelling was mostly from Roy and mostly along the lines of, "I'm not the one knocked her up." The father's arguments were measured, spoken quietly and determinedly. It was evident that the pistol in Roy's hand was the reason he and his sons had not bounded up the stairs for a more physical confrontation.

As other lights came on in the building, the girl and her family climbed back into the car and retreated. The next day, I asked Roy what all the yelling was about. He didn't say much – just that he didn't think he would need the Doc's services.

I don't know whether his girlfriend had the baby or not. There could have been a marriage of convenience to a family friend to provide the child a name, or she could have visited a Crittenton home. Roy wasn't saying. But he did ask me to help him move his cows to another farm, on the other side of Knoxville about 70 miles from the girl's home.

A few months later, Roy graduated and moved to another state. Eventually, the Doc retired – with Roe v. Wade, his services no longer needed.

~~~~~~~~~~

ONE SUMMER SUNDAY NIGHT, when a couple of friends and I were making the cruising scene, we first became aware of Sweet William. We had copped a prize back-row spot at the Pizza Palace, the popular drive-in on Magnolia Avenue. We were enjoying a Super Deluxe (minus the anchovies) while we scoped out the action. The year was 1967 or so.

A white Cadillac convertible, top down, pulled off Magnolia. In the middle of the back seat sat Sweet William, a glitzy blonde female under each arm, an entrance befitting a rock 'n' roll star.

Sweet William, real name Bill Sauls, fronted the Stereos, one of Knoxville's best-known bands at the time. He stood about 6 foot 4, weighed about 260 pounds, and sported shoulder-length red hair and a matching beard. When he wasn't on stage and the weather allowed, he accessorized with a leather vest, which allowed glimpses of the chest rug that matched his beard. Possessed of a raspy, furnace-fire voice, Sauls at full tilt was a perfect bar-room rock 'n' roll singer.

For several years, until his fame led him and the Stereos to the road as an opening act for more established groups, Sweet William and the Stereos were rock 'n' roll in Knoxville.

His regular driver was Sticks, the band's drummer, and, at about 130 pounds, the physical opposite of Sweet William. Excellent at pacing his front man, Sticks knew to keep the Caddy at a stately parade speed as they made the Magnolia rounds. The ritual was a tour of the Palace, then down the alley to the back entrance of the Tic Toc, then west on Magnolia toward downtown to the Blue Circle at Central, and return, with one more stop.

Sweet William's trips always included visits to the Krystal – Sauls had a penchant for sniffing glue, and he claimed that glue sniffed from a Krystal bag worked best.

They were quite the spectacle.

One night a few weeks after that first encounter, I met Sweet William at the Journal. He was an acquaintance of Grady Amann. Both hailed from north Knoxville and had been schoolmates at Fulton High. Sauls would sometimes show up at the Journal seeking publicity, to see if Grady could help. Eventually, after the managing editor banned him from the office as a noisy nuisance, his visits were late at night after the brass had gone home.

By the early 1970s, Sauls and his band were known throughout the southeast, especially in Florida's spring-break spots. They were regulars at the Martinique, a notorious club in Daytona Beach. Another southern group with a large following at the time also played the Martinique, and Sauls was friends with its members. The Allman Joys would later break nationally as the Allman Brothers.

After the Allmans achieved big-venue fame, Sweet William often joined them as opening act. And sometimes they hung out with him in Knoxville. Another Sauls' friend who occasionally visited was Texan Domingo Samudio, better known as Sam the Sham, of Pharaohs fame.

By the time I met him, Sweet William and the Stereos had a well-established and well-earned reputation for on-stage antics, the kind that draws the college-age crowd while driving club-owners crazy. Once, at Bradley's Barn near the

UT campus, a couple of friends and I were seated at a table near the stage as Sauls was working on one of their more popular tunes, the blues standard "C.C. Rider." Hulking over his electric keyboard in full attack mode, he miscalculated on a run of the keys and toppled off the stage, scattering beer bottles and revelers in all directions.

He was helped back on-stage, the keyboard was set back up, and the show went on, bar management nervously making sure the star and his instrument were well back from the edge of the stage. "I'm OK," he told the audience as he sat down. "And, if I need any help, I've got a big jar of uppers, downers, leapers, creepers and crawlers."

The last time I saw him was late one night when he showed up at the Journal. He had, he told us, been hassled by the police as he left the Krystal on Gay Street and needed to duck into the Journal building to establish credibility.

"What were they bugging you for?" we wanted to know.

"They wanted to get me on a weirdo charge," he said with a shrug.

~~~~~~~~~~

AFTER I WAS ESTABLISHED at the Journal – had proved competent at getting coffee orders correct – I was invited to participate in some of the staff rituals. One involved snooker, the pocket billiards game. At the time, downtown Knoxville boasted two poolrooms, both upstairs on the west side of the 600 block of Gay Street. Both were in long narrow spaces, wide enough for only one pool table, but long enough to house eight or nine. The larger of the two, Comer's, had a pair of adjoining rooms and also served those wishing to place sports bets. It was busiest at night. The second, McDonald's, was all about pool and was quieter. The serious, big-money pool games usually were played at McDonald's.

It was there that I first learned about the Knoxville Bear. The Bear was a pool hustler, given name Eddie Taylor. In the world of pocket pool, a world of smoky back rooms, spittoons and illegal gambling, many of the players hid behind colorful nicknames – the Tuscaloosa Squirrel, Wimpy, New York Fats. Taylor picked up his when he was tagged with the moniker after a series of games in Hot Springs, Arkansas. His opponent, after losing his bankroll, said Taylor was as hard to handle as a Smoky Mountain bear.

By the time I heard his name, in the mid-1960s, Taylor was known in pool halls from coast to coast, bringing enough fame to Knoxville to warrant an "official" visit to the University of Tennessee campus. He was invited to the decidedly sterile student billiards room – not exactly a back-room pool hall, but nevertheless the site of well-maintained tables and second home to students who found it easy to cut a math class for a few games of eight-ball or rotation.

I was in the crowd when the Knoxville Bear made his appearance. In dress pants, white shirt and tie, he looked more like a professor than a pool hustler. But there was nothing absent-minded about his demeanor as he made seemingly impossible trick shots and then sank bank shot after bank shot, turning his head before each so that he was shooting "blind." The on-lookers left shaking their heads and vowing more practice, classes be damned.

Eddie Taylor showing students how to shoot pool at the University of Tennessee student center in the mid-1960s. I'm in the back, barely visible on the left.

My reaction, at least for a while, was to start frequenting the more colorful Comer's and McDonald's downtown, places where the denizens were known as Flop, or Butterball or Lefty. There were no exhibitions there – the players were paid not with a check from the university, but with cash from their opponent at the end of each game.

Once, friends and I joined the two dozen or so spectators at a two-day match where more than $30,000 changed hands. The game was nine-ball, $500 on the five and $500 on the nine. The winners were a player from Johnston City, Illinois, and his backer. The losers – one the first day, the other the second day – were a couple of Knoxville's best players, including a pool room owner from the north side of town, and their backers. The Bear was not present – he was out on the road, probably playing big-bucks games of his specialty, banks, in another city.

When the downtown McDonald's closed in 1971, I wrote a story for the Journal about its history. The second-generation owner, J.D. McDonald, told me about hanging out with the Bear, about hosting some of his matches in the 1950s.

As the years passed, and I realized that I did not have the patience required to become a good pool player, I would occasionally read or hear something about the Bear. Pool was beginning to become "legit" with big-money tournaments in Las Vegas and other cities, and the Knoxville Bear and other veteran road hustlers such as Luther "Wimpy" Lassiter and Irving "Deacon" Crane were usually among the finalists.

In 2003, I met up with J.D. again. He and his son were running a room in south Knoxville and selling and installing pool tables. He told me that the Knoxville Bear was living in Shreveport, Louisiana. And he gave me his telephone number.

By then, Taylor was retired. He had seen his game go from clandestine matches in rooms that doubled as bookie joints to glitzy tournaments carried on national television. He had seen women players become TV stars, a long way from the days when they weren't allowed in poolrooms at all.

Maybe the game had become more legitimate than it had been in the days when he made his living at it. But, Taylor said with a chuckle, he had no regrets: "There were times when I was broke and ended up sleeping on a park bench, or in my car when I had one, but I'd do it all over again."

He talked about traveling with and playing many of the game's legends – Crane, Lassiter, Jimmy Moore, Willie Mosconi. And he reminisced about his early days, surviving as a boy in a man's world.

"I dropped out my first year of high school," he said, "because I couldn't stay away from pool. I was always slipping out of school and going to a poolroom. My mother was always threatening to blow them up, but she finally gave in."

Taylor's education came in other ways. "I was playing in rooms in downtown Knoxville when I was about 13 or 14, with men like John R. Cook. He would play me with his overcoat on. Or he'd wear gloves. And he'd win. But in a year's time I was beatin' him even."

It was then that he decided to head up to Morristown for a match with Herman Roddy Jr.

"His dad owned a pool room, and everyone around East Tennessee talked about how good he was. He broke me the first time I played him, then gave me 50 cents for the bus ticket back to Knoxville. I worked on my game for a couple of months, saved my money and went back. Same thing – he broke me again and gave me money for the bus ticket back. But the third time I beat him." Taylor was 15 years old.

After that win, Taylor headed out to surrounding towns, picking up pointers from other players, learning the lessons of the road.

"I went down to McMinnville with a guy named Charlie Brooks. Charlie was a lot older than me, sort of like a second father to me.

"Charlie was a bookmaker, did a lot of football parlays. He got hit pretty hard one week and was really in the hole. He told his customers that if they'd give him two or three months, he'd pay them off. He was an honorable fellow, and they all knew it.

"So he heard about a big poker game in McMinnville and we drove down there. It was summer and it was hot. He found the game, and I found a poolroom, three tables. The owner was also a bootlegger and was drinking moonshine. There was a huge front window, and the sun was coming in, and it was blazin' hot. I wound up beating him pretty good. The wind-up was he gave me a check for $300.

"Charlie did pretty good, too, ended up paying off his bettors. Of course the check from the bootlegger wasn't any good. I learned not to take a check.

"Charlie taught me a lot. People are always asking me how I got into the poolrooms as a kid. It was because I never acted or dressed like a kid. I had been hanging out with adults since I was 8 or 9, when my dad would take me into the poolrooms. And Charlie Brooks taught me to dress respectable. He always wore a suit and tie and a hat. Kids didn't dress like that."

There are many games that can be played on a pool table, and the favorites varied from time to time and region to region. "When I first started out," Taylor recalled, "there were a lot of defensive games, where the objective was to play 'safe' – games such as one-pocket and check. We played a lot of snooker back then. But that changed and you couldn't get any action. Then we'd go to one-pocket or banks. I'd play check all day for a nickel or dime a game. Maybe win $5 for the whole day. Of course back then, that was a lot of money."

As Taylor widened the circle of towns where he could get a game, he learned a better way to make money at the table. He learned to hustle.

"A guy in Lexington, Kentucky, showed me how to lose games on purpose," he said. "How to talk a big game until the money got big, then start really playing. I'd go on about how good I was, how I'd played Ralph Greenfield the week before, and they'd all be laughing at me. They knew I meant Ralph Greenleaf and thought I was too stupid to know his real name. I'd lose and then I'd say, 'Well, I can't really play unless we're playing for big money'.

"It didn't bother me that I was taking their money – I mean, they were trying to rob me, too."

So Taylor made his way from town to town, city to city, hustling in pool halls, relaxing at the horse tracks in places like Hot Springs. Then he found his first big-money tournament.

"It was in 1960 in Macon, Georgia. The guys were all telling the promoter that I was good, that I was as well-known around the South as Coca-Cola.

"There were 10 or 12 players: Willie Mosconi, Ralph Greenleaf, Irving Crane, if you can picture that. But they were playing straight pool and I didn't want that – that wasn't my game.

"By then, my game was banks, which is what they played around Knoxville and Nashville and Atlanta. So I just watched and learned."

The next year, two brothers, George and Paulie Jansco, who owned bars with adjoining poolrooms in southern Illinois, started a tournament. The first was for the game of one-pocket, but by the third year, there was an all-around title as well, involving one-pocket, nine-ball and rotation. And that third year, it was covered by ABC-TV's Wide World of Sports.

"Me and Wimpy Lassiter were in the finals two years in a row," Taylor said. "He beat me in 1963, and I beat him in 1964. That was my first world championship.

"Not long after that they set up a big tournament in this really nice place in San Francisco. Some of the best were there – Lassiter, Jimmy Moore – there were 10 of 'em. You had to win a sectional, then a regional to get in. I was out on the road and didn't have time for that. The wind-up is that I went to the tournament and got a game on the side with a guy from Chicago named Tom Bunch.

"I played him one-handed, $200 a game. One-pocket. Lassiter was in with me [as his backer]. I got it up to where he owed me $800. I asked if he wanted to quit and pay up. He said 'screw you' and we went double or nothing. I ended up winning $6,000. And Willie Mosconi won the tournament and only got $2,500."

By 1967, the Jansco brothers had started the Stardust Open in Las Vegas. There, Taylor picked up his second world championship, as the game continued its move from smoke-filled back rooms to lit-for-television show bars.

Back in Knoxville, Taylor's exploits were making the Journal sports column of Tom Anderson. Taylor remembered a couple of favorite Anderson phrases: "'The Bear was suckering them years ago,' he'd write. I remember once he wrote about me beating somebody, and he said, 'Taylor pocketed the coin.' I thought that sounded great."

Before his age started crimping his game, Taylor and his wife, Violet, bought a pool room in Tampa, Florida, and ran it for several years, hosting players such as Lassiter, Moore and Rudolph Wanderone, known as New York Fats and, later, as Minnesota Fats.

Then, in 1993, Taylor, who had traveled across the U.S. for decades making his living hustling in poolrooms large and small, was inducted into the Billiard Congress of America's Hall of Fame in ceremonies in Kansas City. The hall had been established in 1966, and many of the tournament players had been inducted already. The consensus of the latter-day champions at the ceremony was that it was about time that Taylor made it.

Lou Butera told about playing Taylor in 1962 and the lesson he learned. "He taught me to be humble," he said. "He beat my brains in."

"It's long over-due," Jim Rempe said. "He was my idol."

When I talked with Taylor in 2003, he was still wielding a stick. "My doctor wanted me to teach him to play," he told me with a laugh. He died two years later, age 87.

~~~~~~~~~~~

THE TOP EXECUTIVE, sole employee and chief window washer of the Kalijah Window Cleaning Service was a small-statured, big-voiced character known around town as Squeegee. His unofficial headquarters was the Yardarm, the late-'60s hangout on the northeast edge of Fort Sanders.

Squeegee was also known to the Yardarm's habituees, and to the police, as a troublemaker. He was in the habit of taking a seat at the Yardarm's bar, engaging adjoining barflies in conversation, then, when their backs were turned, drinking their beer. Herschel Peek, the bar's owner, had banned him numerous times.

But bartenders change, especially at college-area joints, and new barkeeps meant unfamiliarity with Squeegee and his tricks. If he stuck his head in the front door and saw an unfamiliar face behind the bar, he would make for an empty stool. And once again be would be a regular, at least until spotted by Herschel or one of the veteran bartenders.

Too, Squeegee had an angel in Danny West, one of Herschel's Clinch Avenue housemates. If Danny spotted Squeegee walking the Strip with his bucket and his cleaning rags, he would offer him a ride to the Yardarm for a beer. Then, after seeing him settled at the bar, he would leave him to his own devices. Afterward, on hearing the ranting of his housemate, Danny would express surprise that Squeegee had been allowed inside the door, let alone given a seat at the bar.

The police knew Squeegee because of his business practices. Riding the bus out Broadway, for example, he would get off with his bucket, his squeegee and his cleaning rags at a likely stretch of small businesses.

Then at, say, a beauty salon, he would go in and offer his services. If no contract was forthcoming, he might go next door and repeat his offer. But, sometimes, depending on his mood, he might argue with the shop owner. He had been known to run his finger down the shop's front window and then turn toward the owner and her customers and say something like, "Lady, that's the dirtiest goddamned window I've ever seen."

Or he might empty his bucket of water onto the inside of the window, recommending that the proprietor clean it herself.

Such behavior would lead to calls to the police and trips to the county jail. From there, Squeegee's behavior often earned him a transfer to Eastern State Hospital, a facility for the insane in west Knoxville.

But the escapade that cemented Squeegee's reputation involved a late-afternoon police raid of a notorious downtown bar. Squeegee was inside when he saw the cops coming through the front door and managed to sneak out a side entrance.

Looking for a place to hide, he crawled under a car, lying on his back between the rear tires, feet sticking out. He then acted like he was working on the differential. Unfortunately, the car's owner was coming down the street, preparing to head home. He climbed in behind the wheel, started the car and drove away.

Squeegee was exposed, no tools, no differential, no credibility to his story. He was then taken to jail, another chapter added to his legend.

For a time, Squeegee was a late-night regular at the Journal where he invariably would pick an argument with one of the copy-desk denizens. One such shouting match ended with the copy editor accusing him of being crazy. Squeegee reached into his back pocket and pulled out a folded, official-looking piece of paper.

"I ain't crazy," he said. "And here's my discharge papers from Eastern State to prove it. Now let's see yours."

Squeegee's friend Danny had another pal who was widely known around Fort Sanders during that period, but stealing beer was not his problem. I'll call him Dean here. For a time, in the winter of 1967, he took up residence in Danny's Volkswagen Beetle. Danny's girlfriend, Cathy Jones, knew Dean from her hometown, Nashville.

Prior to that, he had bounced from couch to couch in various Fort Sanders apartments, staying until he wore out his welcome or until his benefactors moved on.

I met him when he walked into an early-morning gathering at the house where Danny and Cathy resided on Clinch Avenue – his new-found home in its usual parking place at the curb in front. The house was one of those common to the area – once grand before being turned into student housing. But it had not been subdivided; the main floor and upstairs had been rented by Herschel Peek, who had then subleased bedrooms to three of his friends. It still retained vestiges of its former life, including a working fireplace and the airy and loftily tagged "Florida Room" off to one side of the main room.

The space, probably originally a breakfast nook, had been turned into a bar, complete with stools, and that is where we usually gathered and where I met Dean. He suddenly materialized behind a couple of girls sitting at the bar, scaring them when they realized there was a "presence" at their shoulders.

Danny saw him and said hello. Dean only said one word: "Cold." Then he went into the living room and sat in front of the fireplace, where the remains of the evening's fire still smoldered. The Doors were playing over and over on the turntable.

"That's Dean," explained the VW's owner. "He hasn't got anyplace to stay, so I told him he could sleep in my car." The arrangement included shower and bathroom privileges at the house. Fortunately, given the space limitations of the Beetle, Dean was small enough so that he had no problem sleeping while pretzeled into the backseat.

We went back to our business of swapping stories and drinking beer and Dean was soon forgotten. When I crossed the living room headed into the kitchen for another Stroh's, he was still in front of the fireplace, seemingly entranced as settling logs scattered sparks. I took little notice – falling into such states while watching conflagrations was common during that time.

After that first encounter, I would occasionally notice him on the Strip. Unlike many of the late-night regulars seeking "spare change," he never seemed to be hassling anyone. Once, when he saw me in front of the Vol Market, he got my attention with another of his one-word declarations.

"Hungry," he said. I bought him a sandwich, which he took without comment.

Usually, as the night wound down, he could be found waiting for the Volkswagen and its owner to show up, sitting on the stoop of the Clinch house or on the concrete wall in front of the doctor's office across the street.

Like most such Fort Sanders wanderers, Dean had come to Knoxville because of the university. He was from a prominent family, well-known, well-connected, well-fixed. Family plans, according to those who knew him from Nashville, were that he would become a lawyer, or a doctor, or a marketing whiz. But he wasn't on campus too long before school became secondary, and then a dim memory.

Once, I heard later, he was rousted by the cops and arrested. He got "a little bent out of shape," we were told. Conjecture put the blame on "bad acid." Some said LSD was at the root of Dean's problem: "Too much and too much variety." Later, someone who knew him better said that many who had known him in Nashville suspected there was a touch of schizophrenia at play.

Eventually Danny arranged for Dean to get a checkup at Eastern State. He drove him to the hospital and waited while he was questioned and examined. That evening, as we settled into the late-night routine of the Florida Room, Dean's name came up. Danny then told us he had taken him to the center. What happened, we wanted to know. "They kept him," he answered.

~~~~~~~~~~

THESE DAYS, at least in the South, the scenery-clotting billboards encountered on any drive include ads touting now-legal moonshine. The fiery drink's legitimization was quickly seized upon by those who saw the potential for sales. And sales, of course, are what billboards are all about.

But legalization has come with a cost – a serious dilution to moonshine's aura, to its mystique. And I wonder what Kirby, Walden Creek's longtime practitioner of illegal distillation of corn, would make of it.

My introduction to Kirby's product came in the late 1960s – though my consumption ended following a couple of encounters. Actually, the encounters continued, but I refused to drink the stuff after quickly learning why one of moonshine's nicknames is "pop-skull."

A co-worker introduced me to 'shine when he and I visited a bootlegger in Vestal late one night. We then returned to his place in Fort Sanders and were soon joined by two UT football players, one an offensive lineman, the other a stalwart of the defensive front.

Both were the size that their positions demanded. And both were quickly reduced to blubbering fools by the hooch.

I met Kirby a bit later when my friend, his roommate and the roommate's girlfriend – Inga for our purposes here – made the drive up Walden's Creek to Kirby's place. There, Kirby introduced us to his ritual. We sat outside and shot the bull, Kirby taking a keen interest in Inga. Then we sampled his product, a price was agreed on, and the sale was completed.

As I recall, most of the 40-minute drive back to Fort Sanders was taken up by Inga complaining about Kirby being a creep, "a disgusting, dirty old drunk." She refused to accompany us the next time we made the trip.

Decades later, I ran across Kirby again – he showed up as a character in Cormac McCarthy's southern Gothic novel, "Child of God." He was still living on Walden's Creek and still dispensing moonshine.

Though he's now long dead, Kirby's name came up recently when a friend and I, wandering around the hills northeast of Johnson City, noticed one of the moonshine billboards. I told him about Kirby and the trip to Walden's Creek, which is in Wear's Valley just outside the Great Smoky Mountains National Park – in torturous terrain similar to what we were now negotiating.

"Did I ever tell you about my moonshine experience?" he asked. He hadn't, so he did.

"I got a call one afternoon from one of my customers [He's in heavy-equipment sales, describing himself as an 'iron-peddler']. He wanted me to stop by. So I took a company car and drove over to his office.

"He's always asking me to run him to this place or that, so I wasn't surprised when he wanted me to take him 'a couple of miles' up the road.

"Of course, it was about a dozen miles, and it was up this curvy mountain road. We finally pulled off the highway at an old barn, and he told me to wait in the car until he yelled for me.

"He climbed the hill to the house and went inside. I waited. And waited. And waited. Finally, he stuck his head out the door and yelled for me to come on up.

"As I got close, I could hear hillbilly music. When I opened the door, I saw my friend, his buddy and his wife, and a younger woman who, it turned out, was their teen-aged daughter. The furniture had been pulled back and the owner and his wife were dancing.

"With a 'you dance, don't ya?' inquiry, the daughter grabbed me and I was in the middle of the festivities. The jar was being passed around, but by then the rest of them were so drunk they didn't notice that I was faking the drinking.

"After five or six dances, I managed to get my client outside and back to the barn, where he then loaded a half dozen gallon jugs of 'shine into the trunk of my car. Remember, now, this was a company car.

"I headed back to his place, anxious to get shed of both my client and his purchases. Then I noticed a state trooper on my tail.

"When I pointed out that the law was following us my friend stayed calm. 'Pull into the first driveway you see and turn off your lights,' he said. It seemed like miles before we came upon a turn-off, but finally we did. The trooper went right on by.

"'See,' my friend said, 'You were worried for nothing.' But I'll tell you one thing, I haven't given him any rides since – I don't care how good a customer he is." And, he added, "I don't care what the advertising promises, I don't drink any moonshine."

~~~~~~~~~~~

AT THE JOURNAL, cub reporters got their first chance either on the state desk or as the night police reporter, fashioning three-or-four paragraph stories about fatal accidents or shootings. The old hands joked that the duties involved covering the Three R's – rapes, riots and 'recks.

When the state-desk job opened up, after I had put in about six months as a copy boy, the job was offered to me at $55 a week. I would have my own desk across from the state editor, Juanita Glenn. The adjoining desk was occupied by Steve Humphrey, as managing editor, the man who ran the newsroom. The hours were 2 p.m. to 11 p.m. Monday through Friday.

Twice a night I telephoned county jails throughout East Tennessee as well as a handful in southeastern Kentucky and southwestern Virginia, asking if there were fatal wrecks or murders. Though I carried the lofty title of assistant state editor, I only left the newsroom on a story one time – and that was to cover a meeting within walking distance.

For the part of my job involving obituaries, the dead came to me via calls from funeral homes. The callers were, as their occupation required, quietly dignified, with one exception, the owner of a Sevierville funeral home. In a deep, sonorous voice, he always opened the conversation with "Well, I slipped up on one."

Not only was I learning how to quickly compose a story, but I was getting a lesson in Appalachian geography and culture. I soon knew that Chuckey was in Greene County, that Wartburg had nothing to do with warts and everything to do with early German-descendent settlers, that Jellico's Hilltop Tavern was in the news weekly because of brawling, and that Harlan, Kentucky, was one of the most violent areas in southern Appalachia.

In fact, one of the more memorable murders I covered happened not far from Harlan, at a place called Pine Knot. The shooting started during a regular card game that operated out of a building that straddled the state line. It was days before authorities had figured out whether the crime had taken place in McCreary County, Kentucky, or Scott County, Tennessee.

I tried to talk Humphrey into sending me up there for a comprehensive story, sure that I could crack Page One of the Five Star, the city edition. But Ms. Glenn convinced him that she needed me to handle the obituaries.

But I finally made Page One, above the fold, with the story of a late-evening airplane crash in McMinn County – all the reporting done by telephone. Not only did I scoop the competition in Knoxville, but by tying up the party-line phone, I delayed the United Press International correspondent from reaching her boss in Chattanooga. Humphrey was impressed with my thwarting the competition, but I suspect that what he really liked was that I saved the Journal money by talking to several witnesses during one phone call.

While I was on the state desk, I started noticing Jim Dykes' byline. He was a reporter for the competition, the afternoon News-Sentinel. Before long, we had been introduced and, finding that we both possessed a cynical world-view and a disdain for authority, became friends. Soon, we were hanging out at one of his favorite places, a dark, dusty dive on Gay Street about a block away from the newspaper building. It was called Lockett's, and, according to the sign in the window, offered more than cold beer. The place was in the business of "novelties."

And there were numerous things inside that fit that description. The bartender, to start with – he looked as if he had never been exposed to daylight. He didn't say much either, but he didn't have to. There was a parrot, named Polly, that did most of the talking, though the bird had a decidedly limited vocabulary.

But when Dykes was present, there wasn't much opportunity for a parrot, or anyone else, to talk.

I had noticed that Dykes' work was most interesting when the case he was covering tended toward the scandalous. Like most successful journalists of the time, he was quick to recognize the quirks and twists that define the best stories. And he had the chops to deliver the tale in the most compelling way. He could present lurid details in an understated, matter-of-fact way that avoided sensationalism. And, in person, he often had interesting amplification to what he had written.

So hanging out with Dykes typically featured uproarious stories, usually involving him being caught in a dangerous situation involving alcohol. Sometimes, the location would be Cherokee, on the North Carolina side of the Great Smoky Mountains National Park – Dykes was one-quarter Cherokee, and knew many of the tribal characters.

Though he could fit in at the swankiest gathering, I quickly learned that Dykes had more than a passing interest in places like Lockett's. He was soon introducing me to some of his favorite stops, initially in Knoxville, then all over East Tennessee.

One near-by favorite was Opal's Tap Room on Chapman Highway, a sad spot whose owner tried to keep up with the times by featuring go-go dancers.

Dykes believed the effort was commendable and deserved our support, so we periodically stopped in to check out the entertainment, to see if any new ecdysiasts had been added to the bill. We finally gave up – every night we visited there was only one dancer, and it was always the same girl. Good reporters that we were, we introduced ourselves and proceeded to interview her.

She was friendly enough, and since we were usually the only customers paying her any attention, she began to spend her smoke breaks at our table. The first discovery we made was that her name was not Opal. "Well," Dykes told her, "you're still a jewel."

Jim Dykes at Bald River Falls in the mountains near Tellico Plains on a road trip in 2004.

And then there were the roadhouses: bars that were out in the country.

Once, when Dykes and I were driving a back road east of Tellico Plains, he pointed out the weeded-up remains of such a spot, long-since abandoned. "I got in one of the worst fights of my life in there," he said. Of course, I asked what it was about. "I was in no shape to care," he said, adding only that there "were lots of broken beer bottles."

Another time, we had just crossed back into Tennessee from Kentucky, up in Scott County, when we came upon a cinder-block building with a big sign that said "First beer in Tennessee."

"Pull in here," he said, so I did. Then, before he got out of the car, he paused, looking the place over. "You had better go in and get a six-pack to go. If I remember correctly, I'm not welcome here."

Though his notoriety seemed to cover most of southern Appalachia, Dykes was most famous in the joints closer to his Blount County home, including the string of nightspots that ran up what was then state Highway 73, on the stretch from Maryville toward Townsend and the mountains.

One night, exploring the area, we went into a spot that met our criteria: the gravel parking lot featured several pickup trucks, and there was a tasteful neon Pabst Blue Ribbon sign, "tasteful" meaning that it was non-blinking. But when we entered, everything stopped. As non-regulars, we found that we were the center of attention. The bartender, especially, kept looking our way. Dykes was unperturbed, and we found an empty table.

A waitress took our order and things seemed to get back to normal – pool game resuming, jukebox playing, regulars on the dance floor. But when our beers were delivered, the server wasted no time in letting us know that we should hit the highway.

"I don't guess you all want another one," she said, staring hard at Dykes. We took her hint, and made our way out after downing our Blue Ribbon.

We went a couple of miles out the highway to another place. It was quiet inside with only a handful of customers. The bartender served up our beers, and Dykes made the comment that it seemed sort of quiet.

The bartender chuckled. "Yeah, I had to call the law about a half-hour ago, and they arrested four regulars who were involved in a big fight. It's been sort of quiet since."

Of course there were other places where Dykes was welcome. One was the Duck Inn in Alcoa. Long after he had left the News-Sentinel, long after Lockett's had closed, Dykes began writing a column for the Journal called Without a Paddle, where he frequently made fun of his fellow East Tennesseans, especially those who were involved in politics.

It proved popular with the Duck Inn regulars, and they would tell him how he nailed this congressman or that councilman. Once, he and I stopped for a hamburger and beer a couple of days after a column that was a scathingly sarcastic takedown of one of the state's U.S. senators. Two regulars stopped by our table and told him how much they agreed with his support of the native-son politician.

He looked at them, then at me, and said, "I was being sarcastic." They apparently didn't understand what he meant, chuckling before taking their leave.

"Sarcasm, I guess, is wasted in Blount County," Dykes said. "Readers like these make me appreciate Lockett's. At least the parrot had a clear understanding of East Tennessee politics."

~~~~~~~~~~

IT'S LONG GONE NOW, but in the early 1970s, a new Holiday Inn hotel opened on Dale Avenue, just off Interstate 40 and just northwest of Fort Sanders and the University of Tennessee.

The hotel occasionally played host to the famous. One such celebrity occupant for a couple of days in the fall of 1971 was one of Playboy magazine's most popular Playmates – a native of Jefferson County north of Knoxville who was returning to her home turf for a few days.

Not only was June Cochran a playmate, in 1962 she was the magazine's Playmate of the Year. How, you may ask, did a girl from a small town in East Tennessee attain such an honor?

That was the question I put to my Journal boss when I discovered that Miss Cochran was coming to Knoxville as an ambassador of Hugh Hefner's magazine, to grace a car show at the Civic Coliseum. City editor Dick Evans decided to indulge me and agreed that I should interview her and find out.

So, accompanied by photographer Al Roberts, I met with Miss Cochran and her traveling companion, a woman from Playboy who described herself as the chaperone.

The resulting story – with Al's photo – was published in early December of 1971.

What did I find out? How did she escape small-town Appalachia and get to the big city of Chicago and its spacious and ornate and notorious Playboy Mansion? Well, there was an early appearance on Knoxville's Cas Walker TV show with her grandfather, a Jefferson County constable, but it is not likely that Playboy representatives were familiar with the Farm & Home Hour's reputation as a talent showcase. It was Miss Cochran's showing as Miss Indiana in the Miss Universe pageant in Miami that caught the attention of Hefner. (She had moved to Indianapolis with her family after her sophomore year in high school.)

After Hefner found her through the director of the Miss Indiana pageant, Miss Cochran told me, "My mother talked me into posing" for the Playboy photographer.

There followed a reader contest to determine the '62 Playmate of the Year, the magazine's first ever decision to turn the selection over to the readers. In announcing the contest, the Playboy's writer described Miss Cochran as a "silver-haired Hoosier with a modeling-and-movie career in mind." She received, according to the magazine, "the lioness' share of reader votes" with her "perfect blend of little-girl charm and big-girl proportions."

After spending a couple of hours talking with her, I can attest to that description – I was certainly charmed, as was Roberts, who did not want to leave for his other photo assignments.

During my interview, she said that Warner Brothers had offered her a seven-year movie contract, but she had turned it down because of the restrictions it would have placed on her time. But the modeling career move came easy, and Miss December became one of the magazine's most in-demand Playmates.

Reportedly, she was the basis for artist Harvey Kurtzman's long-running "Little Annie Fanny" cartoon strips in Playboy. And, nine years later, she was still representing the magazine at such events as the car show that brought her to Knoxville. She was popular on the auto-racing circuit and eventually married an Indy-car driver. Years later, their daughter became a popular Playboy-online fixture.

One question that I put to her at the time, which did not make the published story, involved the more explicit photos that Playboy's chief competition, Penthouse, was featuring.

"Would you pose nude today, when the pictures are more revealing?" I wanted to know. Her answer echoed the standard answer of the time. It was something like, "Why should we be ashamed of our bodies – that's the way God created us?" Ignoring my arguments, my editor decided against using that part of the story.

When I met a friend from her hometown of New Market in the late 1990s, he told me that Miss December's successful move from the hills of Appalachia to centerfold caused a bit of scandal at the time. But as far as she was concerned when I met her, she had no regrets.

And four decades after her Playboy debut, June Cochran was still a popular former Playmate, easily making the transition to the Internet. When she died in 2003, she had more than 1,000 followers on her Yahoo page.

With Jefferson City native June Cochran. The year was 1971, and though her reign had ended in 1964, she was still doing promotional work for Playboy magazine.

~~~~~~~~~~~

MY ENCOUNTER with a Playmate of the Year made me the envy of several of my friends, especially Lenny, a buddy from high school.

Shortly after my story was published, he woke me about noon on a Saturday, pounding on my Laurel Avenue apartment door to tell me about his almost-meeting with an attractive female in a downtown hotel.

His experience had started with more promise than mine, he claimed. But, he admitted, overall it had not been as pleasant. And, he said, the fault was all because of his accomplice, a mutual acquaintance who was known for head-strong endeavors that could easily have put him behind bars.

"Candler nearly did it last night," he said. Candler (all the names have been changed) was one of Lenny's buddies. We were all two or three years out of high school, and Lenny had spent six months in the Navy until given a medical discharge. I was a junior at the University of Tennessee, and Lenny had just enrolled.

Story was that Candler had spent time in the military because it represented the more attractive of two alternatives given him by a criminal-court judge. He was not exactly college material.

I calmed Lenny, and we got into his yellow Volkswagen Beetle and went to Brownie's on the Strip for a burger – and an explanation. Stories involving Candler were always interesting – if sometimes frightening. Carefully trying to edge the Bug into a spot too small to be designated for parking, Lenny cursed his car. "It was part of the problem last night," he said.

Though he had his own wheels, Lenny was living with his parents a half-dozen miles from my off-campus apartment. And Candler, who did not have a car, had shown up at his house about 9 the night before.

They had made the usual rounds: Blue Circle, Pizza Palace, Tic Toc. After filling the gas tank, Lenny said, he was left with a couple of bucks. Candler said he had five dollars, "So we didn't do anything except cruise." They finally landed a back-row spot at the Palace.

Candler tried talking up a couple of girls, but, Lenny pointed out, it's hard to get much action when you're in a yellow VW.

"Even Candler was striking out," Lenny said, "and you know what a talker he is." He did have a way with the women – until they got to know him.

Candler had decided that he and Lenny should go to a downtown hotel and get a hooker. When reminded that he only had five dollars, he insisted that Lenny loan him his two. With seven dollars, he argued, he could get a room and have enough left to pay the hooker.

The hotel, on a side street downtown, was the kind of place where such transactions were common. Rooms could be had by the hour.

Lenny argued, he said, throwing up "every objection I could think of — but you know Candler." Finally, he told him he would drop him off and then pick him up after a half hour or so. But Candler had another idea.

"I tell you what," he said. "I'll go in, get a room, then go into the bathroom in the lobby and write the room number over the urinal. You come in a few minutes later, tell the bellhop you want to use the bathroom and see what room I'm in and come on up. I'll tell the bellhop to get me a girl."

Lenny again pointed out the obvious shortage of money. "How are you going to pay for the girl?" he asked. "The room cost five. He said he'd figure something out. I dropped him off and found a parking spot on the street. Not a lot of people downtown at midnight."

After he figured that a reasonable amount of time had lapsed, Lenny went into the hotel. "I walked in, nodded at the bellhop and found the bathroom. Sure enough, there was a number written over the urinal. Candler was on the second floor. I walked back out into the lobby and started for the stairs. But the bellhop was wise to that trick. 'You ain't registered here,' he said, and threw me out.

"So I went back to my car and drove around downtown, killing time. Then a cop stopped me. He wanted to know what I was doing. I told him I was supposed to meet a buddy. He told me he didn't want to see me circling the block again.

"I drove to the Blue Circle, made a few circuits, but didn't see anybody I knew. Thanks to Candler, I had no money, so I couldn't even get a Coke. I went back downtown. Same cop pulled me over and told me if he saw 'this yellow Volkswagen again' I was going to jail.

"There wasn't much I could do, so I went home. By then it was after 1 a.m. I figured Candler could take care of himself."

Well, if nothing else, I pointed out, he had a room for the night.

"Exactly. I went to bed. Sometime after I fell asleep, I heard the screen on the window rattling. It's Candler, of course. I'm not about to let him in, so I go out the back door. He's shirtless. And short of breath. And pissed. 'Where were you?' he wanted to know.

"I told him. He cussed the bellhop. And the cop. And the hooker."

So the bellhop sent a girl up?

"That's what Candler told me," Lenny said. "She told him she wanted her money up front. He said he tried to stall her. Turned on all the charm, he said. But he was dealing with Sonya, a girl, he explained, who had seen and heard about everything."

Sonya was an attractive and widely known Knoxville prostitute. And unlikely to be charmed, especially by a cocky 20-year-old.

"So he said she started to leave and he jumped in front of the door. Naturally, she yelled for the bellhop.

"So you still had on your clothes? I asked him. He said he'd taken off his shirt. He was through the door and down the stairs before the bellhop could get from behind the desk. He ran to the Greyhound station on Gay Street and jumped into a cab. The driver took one look at him and asked for cash up front.

"Candler gave him what he had left – my two bucks. That got him a few blocks out Magnolia. He then ran the six blocks to my house."

So you took him home?

"Yeah, but I made him push the VW out of the driveway so we wouldn't wake up my folks. He'll probably come down with pneumonia, what with being without his shirt, and sweating.

He got really pissed when I laughed at him, sitting there in the car shivering.

"When I dropped him off, he swore that he's going to get his own wheels. I told him he'd better, because he wasn't getting into my VW again."

~~~~~~~~~~

A VOLKSWAGEN figured into another story from the same era. In the fall of 1964, the year after Georgia Tech had departed the Southeastern Conference and the football rivalry between the Yellow Jackets and Tennessee was still fierce, two friends and I decided to make the trip to Atlanta to attend the game. We did not have tickets but figured we could get into the game using our smarts, or, as a last resort, buying from a scalper just before kickoff, when the prices were bound to come down.

Atlanta, of course, was a great place to visit – especially for three sophisticated college men like ourselves. We would go on Friday so we could soak up the pre-game atmosphere, check out the action both downtown and around the campus, grab something to eat from the famous Varsity drive-in. The game, like most during that time, was scheduled for early Saturday afternoon.

So we loaded up Britton's Volkswagen and headed south. The third member of the party was Mac, who was 6 foot 2 and used his height as excuse to claim shotgun in the Beetle. The trip down was uneventful, dominated by my grousing about being stuck in the cramped back seat. We had no trouble finding a cheap motel room on the northern outskirts. Then it was on to the Five Points area, the heart of downtown, where we mingled with orange-clad revelers at a bar called the Alibi and where Mac got into trouble with the police – for jaywalking.

After he talked his way out of that, we found a poolroom that had what to our eyes appeared to be a hundred tables. Beer and chili dogs were available in the front room. The rest of the evening is a blur, but somehow we didn't put much effort into finding tickets for the next day's game.

Saturday morning, feeling the after-effects of Friday night, we headed toward the Tech campus and Grant Field. Soon we found ourselves in the same kind of game-day mess that we regularly encountered in Knoxville: crowds of people creating impossible traffic, both vehicular and pedestrian. And we saw no one trying to hawk tickets.

We managed to find the Varsity, but found ourselves unable to stomach the idea of substantial food after the pool-room chili dogs of the night before, and settled on milkshakes. As it got closer to game time, we started debating whether we really wanted to try to get into the stadium.

Couldn't be much of a game, we reasoned, given that Georgia Tech was undefeated, ranked sixth in the country, and a nine-point favorite. Tennessee, which had just switched from the single-wing offense to the T, boasted a strong defense but had been unable to find a player who could effectively handle quarterback duties.

Finally, after some debate, we decided to skip the game and head back to Knoxville. The contest was not on television (few games were back then), but we were sure we could find it on the radio.

So, as we reached Marietta, we caught the kickoff and, heading north, listened as Tech built up a 7 to 3 halftime lead, with Tennessee's defense keeping the Vols in the game. Then, as we neared the state line, and the fourth quarter began with the Jackets ahead 14 to 3, the Vols' third-team quarterback, David Leake, was inserted into the fray.

Leake, whose primary contribution to the team heretofore had been as a kicker, promptly threw a TD pass to Al Tanara. He then led the Vols to another score, and suddenly the Orange faithful saw their team take the lead. We, of course, saw nothing as we Beetled up U.S. 411 into Tennessee. Radio coverage was spotty, with Mac having to constantly work the dial as we moved north. Sometimes we were listening to the work of Knoxville broadcasters, sometimes to Atlanta stations.

But we managed to hear the final minutes as the Vols held on to win 22 to 14, with Doug Archibald returning an interception for the insurance touchdown. After our excitement died down, we realized we could not tell our friends that we had not been cheering for the Orange from our seats in Grant Field, that we had not been present for such an historic upset.

So on Sunday morning we read the newspaper stories, familiarizing ourselves with the pertinent game details, inventing celebratory anecdotes, and then spent the rest of the week gloating in our good fortune at having been at a memorable Tennessee victory over a hated rival. We were obnoxious enough that our friends quickly tired of hearing about The Game. Besides, campus attention was now focused on the upcoming contest.

So we congratulated ourselves for pulling off our own great play – and a trick one at that.

~~~~~~~~~~~

SEVERAL DECADES later, I missed another historic Vol victory. The year was 2002, and I was accompanying one of my long-time friends on his ritualistic game-day circuit.

I had known Rod Harkleroad since grammar school – we had knocked football helmets for a couple of years when we were about 12 or 13. Because we were the two biggest guys of our group, we always did the choosing when teams were picked for backyard games.

When we became semi-organized, with regular Friday-afternoon contests, he quarterbacked the Stompers; I led the Bruisers. We played in the side yard of Danny Meador's house, our only equipment being the ball and, for some, helmets. We imagined our games were the talk of Burlington, the working-class east Knoxville neighborhood where we lived.

Rod had gone on to play high school football, had made all-state as a senior and had received a scholarship to the University of Tennessee. He didn't play much – on the depth chart, he was behind Bob Johnson, now enshrined in the College Football Hall of Fame. But Rod was active in the Vols' Lettermen's Club and kept up with his old teammates.

I was trying to find a different perspective for a story on UT football and had decided that hanging out with the old players prior to a game could work. Rod liked the idea and agreed to get me inside the Lettermen's Club before a game.

We decided on the Arkansas contest because its 8 p.m. kickoff would give us plenty of hanging-out time.

And so we were at Marie's Olde Towne Tavern at 1 p.m. on game day. Despite the gentrified spellings, Marie's was an unremarkable joint on the north edge of downtown Knoxville, with the clientele one would expect from its location only a block from the Greyhound bus station.

But Marie's did sport one thing that no other bar in town did. On the wall was a framed, autographed photo of Harkleroad in full University of Tennessee football regalia. And on this October Saturday Rod insisted that I experience it. "I gave them an exclusive, so it's the only bar in town where you can see it," he explained.

Marie's was our third stop of the day. Rod, after a successful career coaching high school football, was now in the food-service business, and he had pre-game meetings with a couple of clients, providing food for their tailgate parties.

First, we stopped at Steamboat, a sub shop owned by another high school pal, Donny Anderson. Rod had ordered two yard-long sandwiches, fully dressed and sliced into individual portions, and we were going to deliver them to Jefferson County, northeast of Knoxville. After the delivery and back-slapping joking about Tennessee football, we drove back into Knox County, where Rod pulled into the parking lot of a liquor store.

Rod Harkleroad in his University of Tennessee football
uniform, late summer 1964.

"I'm going to let you drive," he said, handing me the keys to
his van. He then mixed Jack Daniels and Sprite in a plastic
cup. "I've got to meet another client at 3 at Riverside Tavern,
so we've got time to stop by Marie's."

After my eyes adjusted to the lack of light in the bar, I found
Rod's picture. He was in full uniform except for his helmet,
looking fierce in a dropback blocking stance. "Nice, huh?"
Rod said. "Enough to make me a regular here."

After we finished our brews and fended off a half dozen entreaties from a beer-begging crone, we left Marie's. "Swamp Rat's on the air by now," Rod said. "And Mrs. Parker needs to call in."

Swamp Rat was Dewey Warren, who played quarterback for UT when Rod was on the team. He now was host of a call-in sports talk radio show. And Mrs. Parker? That was Rod, using his best soft, refined, feminine voice. We got in the van, Rod got out his cellphone and soon had Dewey on the line.

"Mr. Warren?" he said. "This is Mrs. Parker, and I was just calling to discuss the finer points of the game."

The Swamp Rat was a legend among the Big Orange faithful, and Mrs. Parker had become a star of his show, especially on game days. Today, Mrs. Parker wanted to talk about quarterback Casey Clausen.

"I am reminded of breakfast time when I was a child," she said. "We had to be quick if we wanted an extra biscuit. That young Mr. Clausen's holding the ball too long, and that's why the young men on the other side break through, and he gets his rear side blistered. He just needs to be quicker in order to get the last biscuit."

Mr. Warren agreed, thanked Mrs. Parker and turned to another caller.

Mrs. Parker was bang-on in voice and manner; she did not take the game too seriously, and she possessed a propensity for double-entendre that was subtle enough to slip right by Mr. Warren and his producers. The voice disguise was perfect. "You know," Rod said to me after he hung up, "Dewey didn't figure out that I was Mrs. Parker until the third or fourth time she was on the show."

I was now pulling into the parking lot of the Riverside Tavern, a popular spot within walking distance of Neyland Stadium. The Riverside, though it too was a "tavern," had nothing else in common with Marie's. The gameday crowd consisted of the more successful Big Orange boosters. True, some might be as drunk as the old woman we had left at Marie's. And they might be overly friendly, but they were more likely to want to buy a stranger a drink that to try to cadge one.

Rod swapped opinions on the game with his client and then charmed a tableful of Arkansas fans with a "soooie pig."

We then set out on foot for the serious tailgaters, it now being only four hours to kickoff. It was too early, Rod said, for much action at the Lettermen's Club.

There were a couple more client stops and a brief visit with a local politician at his set-up before we made our way to Danny Meador's spot. Danny, my old Bruiser teammate, was now president of an equipment firm and ran the company tailgate at UT games.

Rod and I regularly joined Danny and his company crowd, so we were expected. Another of Rod's UT teammates, Paul Naumoff, would sometimes show up, and they would regale us with football stories. Paul, an all-star linebacker, had spent a decade heading up the defensive unit of the NFL's Detroit Lions before returning to Knoxville. During their college days, he and Rod had roomed together.

One of Paul's favorite stories involved another linebacker, a player who partied with the same abandon that earned him All-American honors on the field. Among the other players, he was also known for his insistence when in search of drinking partners.

"That's the reason I roomed with Rod," Paul would say. "When he showed up at 3 a.m. drunk and rowdy, Rod would start preaching and praying for his soul. After a couple of those sessions, he left us alone."

"But Paul," Rod would add, "I prayed for your soul, too."

The partying linebacker played a major role in another of Rod's escapades, one that was well-known on campus.

Around 1966, word began to spread that a trio of football players had been caught after slipping into the Geography and Geology Building on the Hill in an effort to steal the exam for an upcoming test.

An alarm was triggered, and UT police were soon on the scene. The players panicked and the tight end leading the mission leaped through one of the building's leaded-glass windows. The other two, the linebacker and an offensive lineman, followed. The police then followed the trail of blood from the cuts caused by the glass down the hill to their rooms in Stadium Hall. I don't recall how they were punished, if at all. Rod, the offensive lineman in question, confirmed the story when he and I were talking about it at Danny's tailgate. "But I don't want you all to get the wrong impression," he emphasized. "I wasn't the one doing all the bleeding."

Several drinks and stories later, Rod and I headed for the Lettermen's Club – there was barbecue and it was close to 6 p.m. and we were hungry. Inside, I found what I was looking for – though it was not what I expected. Instead of insights into the TV games or the upcoming UT action, mostly what I heard were complaints about "these young guys not knowing how to play the game" or "not being tough enough to win the head-to-head battles." One of the older complainants' comments, it was obvious, had more to do with racism than anything else, though he tried to disguise it. (The UT football team was not integrated until 1967.) They groused, I took notes, and Rod visited with former teammates.

Finally, it was 15 minutes until kickoff, the Lettermen's Club was emptying, and the noise from the nearby stadium was drowning out normal conversation. We set out for our upper-deck seats.

About half-way up the entry ramp, I realized how tired I was. I was game-dayed out. I looked at Rod, who had been going longer than I had and who had drunk a pint or so of bourbon to boot. He, too, looked tired.

"Do you really want to sit through three hours of football?" I asked him.

Feigning surprise, he looked at me. "You mean you don't want to listen to my insights before each play? And what about all the folks around my seat – they expect me there to tell them what's going to happen."

I had joined Rod at games before, and what he said was true. As soon as the opponent's defense was set Rod would call the play, and 75 percent of the time he was correct. Then he would regale us with derogatory comments about missed blocks and coverage. A game with Rod was always fun.

Once, I asked Rod why he had quit coaching. At his last job, at a rural school north of Knoxville, he explained, he had been forced to lock himself in his office after a night game, because a father angry at his son's lack of playing time was waiting outside. It took a call to the sheriff's office and a deputy's visit to convince the father to leave.

"I decided there had to be a better way to make a living," he said. "Besides, this way I can just tell everyone how it should be done without having to worry about winning or losing." So he stayed involved with the Lettermen's Club, helping out when any of his old teammates needed assistance.

But tonight, he was as tired as I was. We did a 360 on the ramp, Star Spangled Banner blaring in the stadium. We heard the roar of the kickoff as we made our way back to the van and listened to the first few minutes of the game on the radio as I drove back to where my car was parked. Rod assured me that he would sleep in the van until the next morning, his habit after such episodes, and I went home. The next day, I read about UT's victory. Casey Clausen threw a touchdown pass to Jason Witten in the game's sixth overtime. The game ended at midnight.

A few months later, Rod was diagnosed with advanced cancer. But that did not stop him from helping an old teammate. Steve Delong, a two-time All-American who had a career in the NFL, had fallen down a flight of stairs. The resultant back injury left him wheelchair-bound. He was in an assisted-living facility, and Rod was a regular visitor, frequently accompanied by other former teammates, including Elliott Gammage.

"Every week, we'd go see him," Gammage recalled recently. "Steve was angry about his circumstances, but what Rod meant to Steve was unbelievable. Here Rod was dying of cancer, but he had time to visit Steve every week. Rod Harkleroad demonstrated the kind of courage that I pray I'll have when I'm near the end."

A couple of weeks before Rod's death, Danny Meador and I visited him at home. In pain, he was in a lounge chair, his reactions slowed by painkillers. His wife Brenda, a nurse, was at work. A woman we didn't know met us at the door.

"I'm Rod's first wife," she said. "Second," Rod corrected her.

"We couldn't live together," she said with a smile. "But we're still friends."

He turned to us. "It's tough when you're dying, fellas," he said. "They even bring in your ex-wives." We all laughed, finding comfort in knowing that he hadn't lost his sense of humor.

At Rod's memorial service, dozens of former UT footballers showed up. Tales were told, and there was a lot of laughter. One former teammate, Mike Price, repeated a favorite story, one that all the players knew. Rod, Mike, and Art Galiffa, a quarterback on the team during the mid-'60s, were quail hunting one fall.

"We were taking a break, headed back to the trucks," Price said. "Art and I had gotten in front of the others when one of the dogs went on point behind us. I hear a gun go off, and next thing I know I'm on the ground, and blood's going everywhere. They start trying to find where I've been shot, undoing my coveralls. Rod's hysterical. We can't find where the blood's coming from. Finally, I look at my hand and see that a pellet has gone through my thumb.

"Rod finally calms down and we head back to the truck to get a Band-Aid. Rod put his arm around my shoulder. 'You know, Mike,' he said, 'If I had to shoot anyone, I'm glad it was you'."

'Why?' I wanted to know. 'Why not Galiffa – I mean, he's a cocky quarterback'."

"Because," Rod answered, "You're such a nice guy."

Several days after Rod's death, several of his old teammates managed to fulfill one of his last wishes. They slipped into Neyland Stadium and surreptitiously scattered his ashes around Shields-Watkins Field.

"It's good to know," Price told me, "that Rod's there to tell the coaches when they're messing up."

Character Studies

Ben Byrd and other Sports – Fires in the pressroom – Racial realities in the ring – Ace and Big John Tate – River rats and snaked dates – Coeds, and an armed neighbor on Clinch Avenue – Beer and peanuts on Christmas eve

~~~~~~~~~~~

THE MORE-MEMORABLE characters working at the Knoxville newspapers in the 1960s included several talented writers, led by irascible sports columnist Tom Anderson.

Knoxville sports writing is centered on University of Tennessee football, and in the 1950s, Anderson's clear-eyed reporting and smart-ass attitude led to University of Tennessee football coach Robert Neyland banning him from the premises.

And Anderson wasn't popular with Journal managing editor Steve Humphrey, either. In what must have been a unique move, Journal editor Guy Lincoln Smith worked out a deal where Anderson would not come into the office, producing his five-times-a-week column at home and having his wife deliver the copy to the newsroom.

Humphrey wanted Anderson to punch the time clock and spend eight hours a day working from the office; Anderson, no fan of authority in general and the managing editor in specific, did not want to be tied down. (This was long before the use of computers, of course.)

In the seven years I worked at the Journal, I only saw Tom Anderson once – when management brought him in to vote against our effort to unionize the newsroom.

Guy Smith recognized Anderson's talent – and was well-aware that the Journal's sports fans did, too. He had many examples of his columnist's brilliance to cite. During World War II, when Anderson was basically the only person working sports, he would fill the two-page section single-handedly, sometimes rhyming all the headlines. He would send his wife to Knoxville Smokies baseball games to collect the box scores, then write the story himself under her byline – with a decidedly feminine point of view. The account might start, for example, with a description of the hat worn by the woman seated in front of "your reporter."

During one hapless baseball season, he composed a series of fanciful columns about how the Smokies lost a promising pitcher. One of the more memorable was a character he called John the Beachcomber, who wintered on a tropical island and stayed in shape by throwing coconuts – until he was attacked and eaten by cannibals. The columns would end with, "And that's how the Smokies lost another pitcher."

Often, his battles with the managing editor would be over his efforts to slip sexual references into his column. As far as Anderson was concerned he was playing a game with a boss who was much too blue-nosed.

One of his triumphs, though it only made one edition before the managing editor had it yanked, garnered laughs at the expense of a music-minded co-worker. The column had a section about how So and So, while well-known for "tickling the ivories, had also tickled a few organs."

Another column, as written, ended with:

Today's definition:
The verb kumquat, as in
Kumquat on my lap

That one, according to Grady Amann, the final editor to see Anderson's work before it went to the composing room, "never saw ink."

After Anderson's death, Ben Byrd, another talented writer, succeeded him as the paper's lead sports columnist. His weekly free-association picks were must-reads during football season. Typical was the column published the morning of a Vol game with Rutgers, in which Byrd attempted to define a "rutger," finally quoting a fan as saying he wasn't sure exactly what they were, but that he thought they were similar to "yonkers."

While, unlike Anderson, Byrd got along with the bosses, he was known for impatience as deadlines loomed. I witnessed one episode, when piqued by a ringing telephone, he ripped it from the wall and tossed it out the open second-floor window of the paper's Church Street quarters.

But Byrd's more infamous toss happened years earlier when the newspaper was housed on Gay Street, Knoxville's main drag. There, the story went, he threw his typewriter out the window into the alley that runs between Gay and State streets. The incident led to the installation of bars on the windows – not to keep people out but to keep dangerous objects in. Shortly before Ben's 2016 death at age 91, Grady Amann and I asked him about the incident. He said the story had been exaggerated. "It was only the typewriter's carriage," he explained.

In the press box at Neyland Stadium during a game in the early 1970s, Byrd, obviously hung over, disappeared at half time. Midway through the third quarter of a tight contest, he wandered back in, looked down at the field and loudly asked, "Oh, God, are they going to play some more?"

Being the sports-section boss, Byrd did not generally schedule himself to work on high school football nights, an always-frantic three or four hours each Friday during the fall. On one such night, as I was typing away trying to meet a deadline, he wandered into the office, walked over to me, put his hand on my shoulder, and offered this bit of advice: "Chris, in the game of life, there are no winners or losers. The best you can hope for is a tie." Then he got back on the elevator and departed.

In my peripatetic career in journalism, I've worked with (and sometimes against) many characters, but my experiences with Ben Byrd are among those I cherish the most, both because of what he taught me, and because his dry wit made often-onerous tasks enjoyable.

Though many of the Journal's most-interesting characters were denizens of the newsroom, others were scattered throughout the building. One of the more notorious was a pressman named Jerry Miller. No one called him Jerry. He was known as Ace.

I had encountered Ace before I went to work at the Journal, probably in a poolroom, and had laughed at his patter. But it was during my time at the Journal that I really got to know him.

When there were union-management disputes at the newspaper, the pressmen held a strong position – they could hold up the printing of the paper, a major problem for a daily publication. And the pressroom, with its newsprint and the dust that resulted from a massive press running at capacity, provided tinder for dangerous fires.

During my years at the Journal, there were periodic pressroom fires. They would always be small, confined to one corner of the room, but they would always bring both the fire department and lengthy delays of the newspaper's publication.

And they would almost always happen during thorny labor-contract negotiations.

So when I saw Ace, I would jokingly ask him when the next fire was scheduled, just so "I can be prepared to get out of the building." Or, if I ran into him on the street when I was with someone else, I would introduce him as being "in charge of setting fires in the pressroom." He would just laugh and launch into a story, often about his role as a boxing coach/manager.

When I first started paying attention to Knoxville's boxing scene, it was run by a man named Pee Wee – diminutive, as his nickname implied. But Pee Wee could be pugnacious and was not to be messed with. Many of the dozens of kids he had coached swore at him, but most swore by him as well.

As Pee Wee was the gym guy, his counterpart in the money-raising, publicity department was Gene Demont, a former boxer who worked at the afternoon daily, the News-Sentinel, in their marketing department.

The News-Sentinel was a primary sponsor of the annual Golden Gloves tournament, so Demont wielded considerable influence in the area's boxing world. If you got a nod from him, you were OK. But if he considered you what he called a "rinky-dink," then you had a fight to win his respect.

Knoxville drew boxers from around the area – the tournament would pull teams from Chattanooga, Nashville, from Middlesboro, Kentucky, from the Cherokee reservation across the mountains in North Carolina.

One of the boxers drawn to Knoxville by Demont was a middleweight named Jimmy Sullivan, who was from another boxing town, Louisville, Kentucky. Sullivan saw better opportunities for ring victory and Golden Gloves advancement in Knoxville. And Demont got him a job at the News-Sentinel so he could stay in town full-time.

Sullivan and I became friends – both of us were copy boys doing the same kind of errand running. The first time I saw him fight, though my knowledge of the sport was limited, it was obvious that he knew what he was doing. He fought smart.

Though Sullivan and I crossed paths daily, I did not fully comprehend his social situation as an African-American until I ran into him one day a block or two from the newspaper building. He was with a friend, another African-American. He introduced me, and then told me to tell his buddy what he did as his job.

"Same as me," I said, "running errands, taking copy and photos to the composing room and to the engravers, getting coffee for lazy reporters. The only difference is he doesn't have to take the editor home every day like I do."

(The Journal editor, Guy Lincoln Smith, didn't like to drive, so one of my duties was taking him home in a staff car every afternoon. That wasn't part of the job at the News-Sentinel.)

Sullivan grinned at his friend, and said, "See, I told you."

His friend laughed and said, "OK, I believe you; I believe you."

Later in the day, I ran into Sullivan again and asked him what that exchange was all about.

"Aw," he said with a shrug, "he didn't believe I had a job that didn't involve sweeping and mopping." His friend thought he was a janitor and scoffed when he told him he wasn't. For me, the exchange was a small lesson in racial realities.
The Journal didn't cover boxing when Guy Smith was editor – he didn't believe in such a brutal sport. Plus, the News-Sentinel – the competition – was the program's sponsor. But

when Smith died in 1968, the new editor, Bill Childress, changed course, and Grady Amann began covering boxing for the Journal. Often, I would accompany him to the gym, and at tournament time, I was usually ringside.

One year, while Sullivan was still part of Knoxville's team, Demont brought in one of his Chicago friends as an official. Rollie Schwartz was a world-renowned amateur-boxing official, manager and trainer of Olympians. He had worked with such fighters as Cassius Clay, before he became Muhammad Ali, and later with Sugar Ray Leonard. After watching Sullivan, he told Grady that he was one of the best middleweights he had seen.

But Sullivan couldn't overcome the racism of one of the judges in the championship match, losing to a local kid who was white. I was seated ringside with Grady and Schwartz, who shook his head sadly and simply said, "He was robbed."

A couple of years later, after moving to Texas, Sullivan made the national Gloves finals. And, Ace told me decades later, he went on to become a successful optometrist in Louisville.

In 1971, Ace became the main force behind Knoxville's boxing scene when Demont retired. He soon expanded Knoxville's reputation as a nationally known training ground.

Though he had never officially been a boxer – he may have fooled around in the ring a few times when younger – Ace parlayed a keen skill as an observer and his native smarts into a well-deserved reputation as one of the best coaches in the country.

He was a master of promotion as well. Knoxville was soon attracting boxers from other parts of the country who wanted to train with Ace. Success often followed. Ace recognized those with the necessary skills and drive to succeed. And he was an expert motivator.

Olympians Clinton Jackson, Bernard Taylor, Big John Tate, Johnny Bumphus all trained with Ace. But his influence wasn't only with ring skills. At the 2012 memorial service after his death of a heart attack at age 72, testimonials to the things Ace Miller did to keep kids off the streets and off drugs went on and on.

In the fall of 2015, a 90-minute doumentary on Ace by Blake McKinney aired as part of the Knoxville Film Festival.

The movie came about, McKinney told me, when he was talking with his cousin BreAnna Miller, Ace's granddaughter, about "how he touched so many people in and around the Knoxville area.

"I had been telling her about how I would like to make a personal documentary about someone that could tell a good story while also illustrating universal themes.

"We kind of put two and two together and decided to make the film about Ace and what he meant to the people around him."

Part of the idea was the creation of something that BreAnna's children could see to get to know who their grandfather had been. "What we did not realize was that it would serve as a learning experience for BreAnna as well," McKinney said.

"Many of the stories she was hearing for the first time gave her a better understanding of what Ace meant to the community."

As befits a great yarn spinner like its subject, the film includes many tales of Ace – from the east Knoxville boxing gym that now bears his name to boxing matches in New York City, in South Africa, Russia, Finland.

In Helsinki, according to his friend John Anderson, Ace got a hankering for a biscuit like he enjoyed at Ruby's, the longtime Burlington café where he was a regular. So Ace joined the hotel chef in his kitchen and showed him how to make them. For a gregarious storyteller like Ace, there was no language barrier. He was just teaching, like he did with the kids who showed up at the gym.

One of Ace's ring successes was a 6-foot-4 heavyweight named John Tate, who came to Knoxville from his home in west Arkansas to box for Ace.

Big John, as he was soon tagged, was an uneducated African-American with quick hands. He found a job in Knoxville working on a garbage truck, and he went to see Ace, who quickly recognized his potential.

In the 1976 Olympics in Montreal, Big John was the bronze medalist, losing in the semi-finals to eventual gold medalist Teofilo Stevenson, the gifted Cuban.
After turning professional in 1977, Big John went on to win the World Boxing Association heavyweight crown that had been vacated by Muhammad Ali. He held the title only five months, knocked out by Mike Weaver in the 15th round in a

fight that he was leading on points. According to Ace, Big John ignored his advice entering the last round, going for a knockout himself.

Tate's life spiraled downward into drug abuse after he lost the title, and he eventually served prison time for assault and theft.

In 1997, I ran into Tate during a closed-circuit showing at a bar-restaurant in Knoxville's Old City. The bout was the second match between Mike Tyson and Evander Holyfield, the notorious ear-biting battle.

I was leaning against a back wall when Tate walked up. His presence had not been noted during the pre-fight announcements by the bar management even though he was a former world heavyweight champion. We started talking, then, as the fight progressed, Tate began explaining Holyfield's strategy. He obviously knew his boxing.

Between rounds (the fight ended in the fourth when Tyson was disqualified for the ear-biting), I asked Tate what he was doing now.

"Working here," he said, "cleaning the place up when everybody leaves. I've got deals with several places around town." He had come full circle from his days on a garbage truck.

A few months later, Tate crashed his pick-up truck in east Knoxville in an early-morning accident. Two companions were not injured, but Tate was dead. An autopsy revealed drugs and alcohol in his system – and that he had suffered an aneurysm before he wrecked. He was 43.

~~~~~~~~~~

WHEN I DECIDED that I needed more space than my room-and-a-bath could provide, I found a two-bedroom house a few blocks away on Clinch Avenue, on the western edge of Fort Sanders. I had graduated and had gotten a $5 a week raise, so I was feeling flush. And soon after I made the move, I found a roommate, the cousin of Dickson, one of my East High classmates. The year was 1968.

Stanley, as I'll call him here, had been kicked out of the fraternity house along with Tombo, one of his buddies. According to their story, it was because Stanley had snaked the girlfriend of one of their brothers. Tombo contended he had followed Stanley out of the house "to demonstrate solidarity."

Tombo had moved back in with his parents in Fountain City, on Knoxville's northern edge. But he spent most of his non-classroom time at our house, frequently sleeping on the living-room couch, so in reality I had picked up two roommates.

Stanley had been social chairman of the fraternity, and therefore was familiar to Knoxville's beer and liquor distributors. So we decided to turn our dining room into a bar. The distributors, ignorant of Stanley's loss of his fraternity clout, were glad to furnish us with signs, some of them capable of flashing. A couple of cases of beer mugs sporting the Pabst Blue Ribbon logo were added to our haul.

My major contribution was a working jukebox that I had picked up from a friend. We bought a couple of black lights and lava lamps, and Stanley's dad donated his old stereo system. Thanks to Stanley's expertise with electronics, we added speakers until we had 16 scattered through the living room and barroom. We had the best non-licensed bar in the 2300-block of Clinch Avenue.

Using my composing-room connections at the Journal, I printed up membership cards. We called it the Saloon, using wooden-block Studhorse Stymie type I discovered in a little-used printers' cabinet. (Officially, the font is named Cooper Black.) It was probably the first use of the blocks since the 1920s.

After the cards were handed out to the frat brothers of Stanley and Tombo, the Saloon was soon a topic of conversation on campus. And people were showing up at our house on Friday and Saturday nights who I had never seen before.

I was working a Sunday-through-Thursday shift, leaving the newspaper at 2 a.m. Friday and returning at 5 p.m. Sunday. My car was a Mark I Jaguar sedan, and Stanley was driving a red Sunbeam Alpine convertible. My half of the rent was less than $50 a month with utilities adding $10 or so. We were in the middle of a college community; we had money (or at least I did) – and it was 1968, when college life was tumultuous, which translated as exciting.

Behind our well-equipped, neon-lit bar at the Saloon, about 1969, proudly wearing my Budweiser vest.

Three girls, students all, moved into the house across the street. Add the females I knew, the connections of Stanley and Tombo, the single staffers of the Journal who hung out with me and Grady Amann, and a Saturday night at the Saloon was full of promise, the alcohol plentiful, the music loud. If the windows were open, the jukebox could be heard two blocks away on the Strip.

Because I was single and worked at night, the house also became popular for dinner-hour trysts as long as Stanley wasn't home. Because we were on a dead-end street, and Stanley's car was a red convertible, it was easy to tell when he was absent. Somehow, embarrassing encounters were kept to a minimum.

One of my most memorable unannounced returns wasn't embarrassing at all as far as I was concerned. I got home from an out-of-town trip about 3 a.m. to find the house dark and quiet. And, when I opened my bedroom door, I found two girls asleep in my bed. One I knew; the other was her dorm roommate. Fortunately, the bed was king-size and they made room for me. The next day, I made sure that word of the arrangement got around.

We took to defining a successful Saturday-night party by the number of people who were asleep around the house on Sunday morning. If there were at least two who were strangers to both Stanley and me, then we deemed it a resounding success.

One I remember, discovered asleep on the living room couch, was a girl who claimed to have been a bunny at the Playboy Club in Atlanta. She certainly looked the part.

Other female guests at various times included the two concurrent girlfriends Stanley tried to keep from discovering each other, a girl named Tex being pursued by Tombo, the daughter of a Ford Foundation official who had grown up in India, an innocent from Alabama whose dad was a chicken-raising magnate, a brassy, red-haired Pennsylvania girl who went on to a successful career in law, and the Nashville cutie who dropped out and went to San Francisco during the Summer of Love.

And there were the two skaters with Holiday on Ice who Stanley and I met at a hotel bar downtown. (For several years, the ice show put their production together each summer in Knoxville.) Cammie was from Montreal and was

great fun. Unfortunately, I only knew her for one weekend –
early Monday morning the troupe left for Boston to open
their season.

If Cammie and her cognac tastes exuded glamour, other
regulars were more representative of the times: girls who
favored gypsy-style dress, cheap wine and marijuana.

One of the latter talked me into climbing into the empty
boxcar of an idle train on the tracks a half-block from our
house one Saturday night. Initially, we found the setting
exciting and romantic. Fortunately for us, before the train
started to move one of her friends found us and steered us
back to the party.

One of our across-the-street neighbors was a frequent visitor
to the Saloon. I like to think it was because May found the
setting interesting, if not exciting. But it probably had more
to do with proximity and the fact that she did not have a car.
As far as I was concerned, she was always welcome – May
was smart, self-assured, un-impressed by Stanley's too-cool-
for-school frat friends and un-afraid of trying the weird
alcohol concoctions we created. She was more mature than
most of her peers, and I enjoyed her company.

She also would tip me off when Stanley was preparing one of
his clumsy attempts to convince me to fund his partying. As
far as she was concerned, Stanley and his friends were
clowns not to be taken seriously.

A few years later, I saw her for the last time a half-world
away in a small town in Germany. The memory is of dancing
in the upstairs live-music room of a gasthaus while her

boyfriend drank with friends downstairs. There was then a drunken return to their apartment in the next town over twisting, narrow roads, the boyfriend driving while May and I sang love songs of the 1930s. He was either too drunk to notice the lyrics, or too diplomatic to acknowledge our lack of discretion.

~~~~~~~~~~~

AT SOME POINT during my Clinch Avenue sojourn, I acquired a four-man inflatable canvas raft for the purpose of taming the white-water rapids of the nearby mountains. Tombo bought a two-man version and we frequently put together groups for weekend jaunts.

Inflated, the four-man could be tied to the top of my car, announcing to whoever saw it that the occupants were white-water enthusiasts. When Tombo was along, his raft would be tied to the top of his car, an early-'50s Pontiac compliments of his grandmother. It was distinguishable because the driver-side door wouldn't open – he had to enter and exit from the passenger side and slide across the seat to get under the steering wheel.

There were several memorable trips before raft air leaks and new interests put an end to our river-running episodes, with three that stand out. Two involved water; one did not.

The first was to Leatherwood Ford, a put-in spot on the Big South Fork of the Cumberland River 70 miles northwest of Knoxville. The takeout was about 25 miles downstream near the town of Stearns in Kentucky. There was a torturous dirt road to an old coal-mining facility called Blue Heron where we could leave one car for the drive back to Leatherwood Ford.

Late one night at the Journal, five of us convinced each other to take the trip. Pittman, a copy editor, and Horne, night-police reporter, were both prone to bull-headedness. The third, Stokes, lived in a cabin on Watts Bar Lake and was a veteran of canoeing. Wilson was the night-shift Associated Press correspondent, a native of Washington, D.C., and completely ignorant of East Tennessee's terrain.

We decided to set out the next night when we got off work. (Stokes was the only non-newsman in the group, but he was a night-owl like the rest of us.) That meant we would leave Knoxville in two vehicles at 2:15 a.m.

After a stop for breakfast along the way, we figured we should get to Stearns about daybreak (we wanted daylight for the dirt-road trek to Blue Heron). We would then leave a car at the abandoned coal facility, then drive back south to Leatherwood Ford to put in. End of the day would see us back at Blue Heron, tired, wet and triumphant.

We made Stearns, then Blue Heron, where we took photographs to prove our presence. One vehicle was parked before we headed to Leatherwood Ford.

There we beheld an ominous sign – someone had propped a seriously bent aluminum canoe against a tree at the put-in, a silent warning about the potential of Big South Fork.

Horne and Wilson and inflated raft at Leatherwood Ford,
shortly after we wisely aborted our river trip.

But on this day, we quickly noticed, there was not a lot of
water in the river. In fact, the stream was only a series of
small pools connected by trickles. Horne, walking
downstream, called for us to follow him. "We can put in
here," he said. "There's plenty of water here."

He was right – but the water was not moving. Undeterred, he
and Wilson wrestled the four-man raft out of my dad's
station wagon and into the water. After adding a cooler full of
beer, they paddled a few strokes before running aground in
the shallow pool. Stokes and I searched downstream for
more water without luck.

Pittman, already realizing the hopelessness of the situation,
shook his head. "This isn't going to work," he said.

The arguing started. Horne and Wilson contended that we should head downstream, that we were sure to find a raging stream just around the bend.

Stokes and I answered that they were crazy, that Blue Heron was 25 miles away, and that we could not hike that far in one day, especially since we would be pulling two rafts around rocks and logs. Finally, Pittman suggested that we turn the large raft over to Horne and Wilson – after they had given us instructions about what to tell their next of kin – and then drive back to Blue Heron to wait until dark, at which point we would return to Knoxville bearing the bad news. Wilson was married – his wife would be despondent, Stokes pointed out. And, he insisted to Wilson, "I'm not going to be the one who tells her that the last thing we saw was you trying to push the raft off rocks while ankle deep in the river."

"I'll take pictures so she'll at least have that," I added helpfully.

Cooler heads prevailed, and we recovered the second car from Blue Heron and headed back to Knoxville. We had to listen to Horne and Wilson grousing on the return trip until, after a couple of beers each, they fell asleep.

The second episode, a couple of months later, involved me, Horne, Stokes and Alice B. Toklas brownies. Perhaps remembering the trip to the Big South Fork, our plans this time were less ambitious. As I recall, the decision was made after the brownies had been consumed.

We decided to take the four-man to the Little River, south of Maryville just outside of Great Smoky Mountains National Park. The four-man had two air-chambers, and we decided not to inflate it until we were ready to put in. That way it would fit into the back of the International Scout I had acquired.

We got to the river without problem, unloaded the raft and screwed the pump into one of the air chambers. It was soon inflated. Then we discovered that we had been so successful at screwing the pump into the connector that we could not un-screw it. And, we soon realized, we had no tools that might have helped us get it un-screwed. Plus, thanks to the brownies, none of us was functioning at 100 percent.

After about an hour of wrestling with the pump, with frequent beer breaks, we gave up. Since we could not unscrew the pump to let the air out of the one chamber, we then had to stuff the half-inflated raft into the back of the Scout. Once again, our white-water trip had to be aborted.

If we failed in our attempts at river adventure, we could at least put up a credible front. That's what Stanley and I decided one summer Saturday afternoon. Horne was throwing a party at his place several blocks away.

So Stanley and I inflated the four-man and strapped it to the top of my car. Then we changed into shorts and t-shirts and went to the party. We had, we told everyone, spent the day in the mountains, besting the rapids of the Pigeon River.

No one questioned us. And at least one female was impressed. Her name was Chloe, and she was a stranger to

Stanley and me. But her date, who was driving a Corvette, had parked just behind my Jag, and she had entered the party wanting to know who owned the raft on top of the car. Someone pointed to the two guys drinking Champagne Velvet beer – Stanley and me. (When most everyone else on campus was drinking the latest beer craze – Stroh's – we opted for CV because it was bad-tasting enough so we didn't have to worry about others stealing it at parties. Plus, it was cheap.)

An hour of so later, the driver of the Corvette walked up and asked me if I had seen Chloe. He couldn't find her. A search was conducted, and finally she was located – on top of my car, in the raft with Stanley. The snaking of Chloe was, in retrospect, probably the greatest triumph of our East Tennessee rafting efforts.

But in 1971 a female friend and I joined an eight-day, seven-night raft trip down the Colorado River through the Grand Canyon. We were part of a group of 30 occupying two rafts manned by professional guides. It was a memorable experience – bone tired and cold when the sun disappeared behind canyon walls around 4 p.m., but raring to go at daybreak the next day. There were bucking rides through treacherous rapids and hikes up side canyons with spectacular scenery.

But the trip also marked the end of my relationship with my companion. And it made the river trips around Knoxville boring. The raft was soon traded for a half-gallon of bourbon.

White-water rafting on the Colorado River in 1971.

~~~~~~~~~~~~

LATE ONE MORNING in 1969 I was awakened by a persistent knocking on my front door. A quick glance through the bedroom window revealed an official-looking sedan on the street.

I went to the front door and found two men in suits. One asked if I was Christopher Wohlwend. I answered in the affirmative and then said, "How can I help you?"

They identified themselves as being from the University of Tennessee police department. I told them that, having graduated, I was not a UT student. Sheepishly, they then explained that the woman who lived next door had been calling the home of the university president, Andy Holt, complaining that her UT-student neighbors were spraying pepper into her house.

There was only one more house on Clinch Avenue before it dead-ended into the berm supporting the railroad tracks that crossed the neighborhood before ending on the southwestern edge of the university campus. Only a shared driveway separated my house from that of the elderly widow who lived there.

They then asked if I minded, to humor my neighbor, if they came inside for a few minutes.

I let them in and explained that my roommate (Stanley was at home in Nashville at the time) was a UT student, and that the neighbor (I'll call her Mrs. Pollard) was always throwing crazy accusations around the neighborhood. She had taken a particular dislike to Stanley when he had moved in a couple of months earlier.

There were nods from the two cops; she had been calling the department with various complaints for several years. But, they added, somehow she had recently obtained Dr. Holt's home phone number, and the situation had gotten out of hand.

After a few minutes, the officers departed, and I escorted them down the sidewalk – an effort to ensure that my neighbor saw that they had made an official visit to 2303.

Mrs. Pollard's conflicts with her neighbors had escalated a few months earlier, when the young couple who lived in 2301 heard what they believed was a gunshot and saw their cat hightailing it back home from the direction of Mrs. Pollard's backyard. She was standing on her back stoop with a pistol.

A shouting match ensued, and I was informed of the suspicion of Mrs. Pollard's being prone to gunfire shortly after I moved in.

She confronted me – without any visible weaponry – within a month after I took up residence. The party marking my move-in produced a crowd, and, thanks to the jukebox and our sound system, the music was loud, helping broadcast the raucous celebration.

Mrs. Pollard yelled at the guests who were on the front porch, then called the police. Two officers arrived and advised me to keep the party inside.

From then on, Mrs. Pollard saw to it that the black and white city-police car was a regular visitor to 2303 on party nights. In fact, on one visit, the cops told me that they had added my house to their regular weekend beat.

Upset as she became when we were partying, Mrs. Pollard was not shy about asking me for help. And that led to a reversal of the usual confrontation – I sent the police to her house.

One afternoon, she knocked on my door and asked if I would help her flip the mattress on her bed, as it was too heavy for her to do it by herself. So I followed her over and into her bedroom. On the nightstand next to her bed was a .38 revolver, bullets visible in the cylinder.

The next day, I informed one of my co-workers at the Journal, the city editor, who was married to a policewoman who was familiar with Mrs. Pollard. She paid her an unannounced visit and saw the .38. Mrs. Pollard was warned about firing it. She denied that it ever left her bedroom, insisting that it usually stayed in the drawer of the nightstand.

I was told about the visit and the pistol and warning. But Mrs. Pollard continued the pepper-spray accusations against my roommate. Finally, deciding to get serious about graduating and wanting to escape the partying we had created with the Saloon, Stanley moved out. Mrs. Pollard then advised me not to get another roommate. I did her one better by moving out, away from campus.

After I returned to Knoxville in 1994, I drove by 2303 on a warm Saturday afternoon – judging by the group on the front porch, it is still residence to students. And Mrs. Pollard's house had gained a couple of ungainly, tacked-on additions since the late '60s – I assume the present owner decided to do as the other neighbors and provide housing for UT students.

I didn't hang around to see if the police were still regular visitors.

~~~~~~~~~~~

BY THE TIME of my move to Clinch Avenue, I was a regular at the Yardarm Tavern, a bar on Forest Avenue at the intersection of 11th Street, in the far northeast corner of Fort Sanders.

Within a short time after it opened, the Yardarm became a popular hangout. University students living on that edge of the campus' residential spillover found it convenient, as did residents of what remained of McAnally Flats, the area of blue-collar neighborhoods and warehouses that had been isolated by the interstate-highway expansion just to the north. The building was within walking distance of both groups.

The clientele combination, incongruous as it may have seemed, bred success, and over the course of the next couple of years the place would go through two expansions, the first adding space for pool and ping-pong tables, the second adding a room with tables and chairs.

The growth had little effect on the regulars occupying the barstools, especially the holdovers from the original space's predecessor, a short-lived joint called Haynes Bar.

When I took a seat at the bar, I was served by Bob Selwyn, who with his girlfriend, Annie Porter, drew the beers, tried to maintain order and sometimes provided solace. Eventually, they expanded the place's menu, adding a cosmopolitan flair with tacos and slices of lasagna that they made at home, wrapped in foil, and brought in to sell.

Before, the menu had been limited to peanuts in the shell or cheese and crackers. "Five rectangular pieces of American cheese and five crackers, 25 cents," Selwyn recalls. "No more and no exceptions."

"There weren't any Mexican restaurants in Knoxville then," Selwyn says. "I like to think I introduced Knoxville to Mexican food with my tacos."

Tasty as the two-for-50-cents tacos were, I usually opted for the lasagna, a generous portion for the same price – but more filling. At happy hour, draft beer was 15 cents a mug.

Selwyn was hired by the Yardarm's owner, Herschel Peek, in December of 1966. "A friend, Mike Baughard, was working there, and I had helped him out a few times after another friend, Joe Anderson, got married and quit," he says. "One night Herschel walks in and asks, "'Who are you?' I told him, and he hired me to take Joe's place as a bartender."

"The pay was 87 cents an hour – I don't know how he came up with that figure. Four p.m. to midnight, Monday through Friday, sometimes Saturday. That schedule allowed us to continue as full-time students at UT.

"Annie was just about always there, too, but she was never an employee. We kept what we made on the tacos and the lasagna."

Selwyn remembers one of the Grand Avenue regulars as being particular about where he sat and what he drank.

"Tex would come in about 5 and sit at the end of the bar. I had to have a bottle of Schlitz and a warm mug at his place by the time he got to his seat. So I'd keep my eye on the door for him every afternoon. Sometimes, I'd have to chase someone off his barstool when he'd come in. And occasionally, he'd get so drunk I'd help him walk home – only about a block away at one of the rooming houses on Grand Avenue."

Selwyn was so important to the bar that his absence led to Herschel locking the door on a Saturday in the spring of 1967. The explanatory sign said "Closed: Bartender is getting married." It probably didn't matter to most of the regulars – they were helping Bob and Annie celebrate their nuptials.

As the activism of the Sixties began to ratchet up, given its proximity to the UT campus and its generally rowdy reputation, the Yardarm was soon attracting the attention of Cas Walker and other right-wing Knoxville politicians. For a period, an unmarked police car and its occupants would be stationed in the parking lot across the street. Many of the regulars would wave to the cops as they entered or exited. And, for a time, the cops would regularly come in to ID check for underage drinkers.

If Cas had braved the Yardarm's notoriously filthy bathroom, he might not have been so suspicious. The most prominent graffiti, speaking to politics as well as the frustrations of the grad-student author, read: "Fuck Communism and remote sensing."

A couple of years after Selwyn's tenure had ended, one of his successors figured into another Yardarm police story.

Rusty Brashear remembers it being a football-game afternoon. "Quite a crowd had gathered in front," he says, "and, though it was basically peaceful, Forest Avenue was blocked.

"The police were trying to clear the street, and they arrested one of the regulars for public intoxication. They didn't cuff him, just put him in the back of one of the cruisers and closed the door. Then something else drew their attention, and another celebrant opened the car door so his friend could escape. He scrambled down to Grand Avenue and disappeared."

One of my last Yardarm experiences happened due to would-be burglars who had been causing more serious problems attempting to break in. Herschel asked Grady Amann and me to spend Christmas Eve in the bar – door locked – making sure no one tried to get in.

We were to be paid in all the beer and peanuts we could consume.

Though the front door was tried a couple of times by passers-by who noticed the lights inside, we had no trouble. Our biggest problem was trying to stay upright when we wobbled out about 8 a.m. on Christmas morning after a long night of beer and peanuts.

Leaving Campus

Sleeping in bear country – A mountain man and marijuana – The Wall of Death – President Nixon at Neyland Stadium – Carp Surprise and other antics in Society – Fire in the newsroom – The two-gun bookie – Mystery at Brother Jack's

~~~~~~~~~~~

EVENTUALLY, the partying at 2303 caught up with me. More than once on weekend nights, I answered front-door knocks to face UT students I did not know: "We heard there was a party here at the Saloon."

If Stanley was around, I could turn the guests over to him and leave, escaping to the Yardarm or to Bill's Barn, the open-all-night restaurant in Bearden.

On one such night, I returned to a wide-open front door, music blasting. No one seemed to be home, though Tombo's car was out front. After turning down the music, I went into the bathroom and discovered Tombo passed out in the tub, covered with a soaking-wet quilt.

Later, Stanley's girlfriend told me that they were trying to sober him up and left him in the tub after wrapping him in the quilt and turning on the shower. The next day, though Tombo seemed no more hung over than usual, I began to see that maybe the partying at the Saloon was becoming problematic.

Plus, my main escapes became known as likely places to find me – I was being called to the phone at both the Yardarm and Bill's (this was before cell phones) – usually the caller wanted to know if anything was going on at the Saloon, though sometimes it was one of Stanley's girlfriends searching for him.

So, when the weather was warm, I would occasionally opt for an old favorite getaway. I would drive south to U.S. 129 and head up into the mountains.

The highway skirts the southern edge of Great Smoky Mountains National Park and is now famous as the Dragon, known to motorcyclists around the world for its curves. Then, it was simply a remote and dangerous highway through the mountains.

I favored a spot overlooking Calderwood Lake where there was a picnic table hidden in the trees. With a sleeping bag that I kept stashed in my trunk, I could spend a restful few hours. The only potential problem, which had not occurred to me until I was awakened by a snuffling noise, was that I might attract the attention of a curious bear. Fortunately, my yell scared him off.

Back in my Boy Scout days, I had spent a lot of time in the mountains, both in the park and in its surrounding national forests. There was camping in Cades Cove and on Big Creek, hikes up Bluff Mountain, and, later when I had a driver's license, hanging out with Gatlinburg friends in the popular resort town.

I had even discovered that a distant ancestor had successfully mined for gold in an area just south of the park known as Coker Creek. My brother Ben and I found two of the three adits that he had worked, and, though we never found gold, we did find evidence of recent claim jumpers.

~~~~~~~~~~

IN 1992 I DROVE U.S. 129 again, this time not seeking a hiding place but a story, a profile of an interesting Smokies native. Roaming the South for The Atlanta Journal-Constitution, I had heard about a retired national-park ranger named JR Buchanan. He turned out to be one of the more intriguing characters I met during my newspaper days.

JR Buchanan (his given name was just the initials) was a native of an area known as the Canes. I had arranged to meet with him at his home in Happy Valley, just outside the southern edge of the park, not far from the Canes and not far off U.S. 129. There, I spent several hours listening to fascinating stories of his treks through the mountains in search of poachers, lost hikers, and in one of his most perplexing cases, the skull of a slain Florida man.

He knew where the body should be – on the rocks alongside Walker Prong, high on Anakeesta Mountain in the park, a couple of miles from the nearest road. The victim had been taken from his car weeks earlier by two murderous companions.

And Buchanan soon knew why the body wasn't there. Animal tracks crisscrossed the sandy spits along the creek, the prints of "five or six different bears."

Then Buchanan and his partner, Buck Branam, found a jawbone, a human jawbone. And, in the still eddy pools of the creek, they spotted bits of what looked like skull.

"The bears had gotten the body and tore it apart, carrying it off. They'd cracked the skull open to eat the brains," Buchanan told me, relishing the detail.

The year was 1981, and Buchanan and Branam were rangers, back-country specialists brought into the case after one of two suspects told the FBI his companion had taken the victim up the creek and killed him with a blow to the head.

"We had to have the skull to prove the murder," Buchanan said.

So he and his partner got down on their hands and knees to look for signs of bear.

"The rocks were covered with moss – we would lift the moss and feel underneath for the imprints on the bottom. We worked our way up the side of the ridge from the creek – crawling – looking for anything unusual."

Buchanan's specialty was looking for things unusual: He was trained in his youth by his grandfather and uncle to track game through the forest. And if you can track bear, turkey and deer, you can track people: poachers, lost hikers, marijuana growers, murderers.

The "unusual" might be a broken twig, an overturned rock, the silvery underside of pine needles. It this case, it meant the cracked and yellowing remains of a human head.

"After we'd crawled around for about four hours, Buck spotted the skull," Buchanan told me. Later, forensic examination revealed a fatal blow to the head, "just like the man described it."

So Robert Elton Taylor, 29, and Freddie Ray Staton, 32, went to the federal penitentiary for the murder of Albert Brian Hunt, a 20-year-old Floridian who had befriended them in a park campground.

When I met him, Buchanan was 65 and retired to the house he and his wife Phyllis built in Happy Valley. Dressed in camouflage – his "back-country" gear – and smoking one cigarette after another, he told me his story quietly in the speech of East Tennessee, with its flat drawl and idiosyncratic syntax.

He is slight, what might be called wiry, built that way, says former co-worker Bill Acree, "on purpose, so he can get through the brush faster."

Self-effacing, Buchanan calls the late Branam, the "best tracker I ever saw." But Acree and others who have worked with him pin that label on Buchanan.

The Buchanan house is tucked into a fold at the foot of Chilhowee Mountain. A few hundred yards away is the western boundary of the half-million-acre wilderness of Great Smoky Mountains National Park – Abrams Creek and

Hannah Mountain, Whistling Gap and Parson's Bald, Tater Ridge and Sheep Wallow Knob – Buchanan's country.

The high ridges, hollows and coves of what became the park were Buchanan's back yard when he was growing up in the valley. He refers to deep-woods landmarks like they were street intersections. "Between the Jumpoff and Charlie's Bunion," he might say, or "just above Greenbriar."

His grandfather Tom Hearon and uncle Jerry Hearon were trappers and hunters in the mountains. They were, he said, "old-timey mountain men."

"They hunted back when hunting was something they had to do to eat," Buchanan said. If a deer had been wounded or a fox had dragged off a trap, the men would read the signs and follow – bullets and traps weren't to waste.

From his grandfather and uncle, Buchanan had learned the lore of the woods by the time he enlisted in the military in 1944 at age 17 to serve in demolition crews with Gen. George Patton's 3rd Army. He still puts the training to use, he told me with a sly grin. "I like to play around with explosives," he said.

When burglars broke into his house while it was being built and carted off his new appliances, he decided it wasn't going to happen again. He devised his own protection system.

A hand-lettered sign addressed would-be thieves and was still posted on his outside wall: "Warning. This house is booby trap with C4. Befor you enter please have a long talk with God."

The system he used on his truck was less extreme: He connected a stun grenade to the ignition when parking it on fishing treks.

After the war, Buchanan worked a variety of jobs – "weren't none of us interested in settling down right away" – before joining the National Park Service in 1954.

Soon he was putting his tracking skills to use, helping to search for hikers and campers who had wandered off trails into the thick, laurel-choked forests. And working back-country against poachers and trappers.

"I'd walk the park's boundary 12 to 15 miles a day, five days a week," he said, "looking for any sign that someone had gone in." Poachers would slip into the park after black bear, deer, turkey, fox, mink, ginseng.

Many, like Buchanan, were local mountain men, ("I've arrested plenty of my friends," he said.) They knew the woods, too. And if they were hunting game, they were carrying rifles.

"The poacher's always looking over his shoulder. Tracking 'em, I'd mostly zigzag," Buchanan said, "because they're liable to put a high-powered bullet through you. You try to figure out what they're hunting for and beat 'em to the place they're going."

Experienced poachers know how to avoid leaving tracks. "They'll go through a lot of rocks. They'll deer-walk [lifting their feet straight up and setting them straight down] so they don't scuff up any pebbles or leaves. They'll back in.

"Once I got so close to a poacher who had set up for a deer that when he pulled his wristwatch up, I could tell it was exactly 1:15. And he still didn't know I was there.

"I'd lose a track now and then, especially an old poacher. Usually where they'd mess up is with the cobwebs early in the morning. If the cobwebs were broken, I knew somebody'd been through there."

Sometimes he had help.

"There was an old-timer, I caught him digging ginseng. 'I guess I've been caught again' he said. 'How'd you know where I was'?"

" 'Your friends told me,' I said.

" 'My friends'?"

"The crows – they come all the way down that hollow with you'."

Then there were the elusive and dangerous wild hogs. The European wild boar, a sharp-tusked, nocturnal animal not native to this country, proliferated in the mountains after escaping from private hunting preserves outside the park in the 1950s. Using their tusks, they tear up habitat for deer, bear, turkey and other native species, destroying rare, deep-forest plants as they root.

Park rangers are directed to kill them.

"They're dangerous when they're hit," said Buchanan, "and they can carry a lot of lead. If you've wounded one, you've got to track it down and kill it.

"It'd be kind of scary sometimes – you'd get within 10 or 12 yards of one, and here he'd come. Their eyesight's bad, but they've got a sharp nose on 'em."

The marijuana growers came along in the late '60s and early '70s, using the park because the high tree cover prevented crops from being seen from the air. They also didn't want to risk their land being confiscated if they were caught.

The northwestern edge of the park is bordered by an area of Cocke County called Cosby, which retired Knoxville FBI agent Bob Swabe described as "the moonshining capital of the state." Moonshiners who switched to marijuana brought along sophisticated ways to hide and protect their products.

"They'd boobytrap their trails," said Buchanan, "sometimes with trip wires and sometimes with snakes. "I've run across where they'd have copperheads or rattlesnakes with their tails tied to stakes with ropes. Being tied down like that, those snakes'd already be mad."

Poachers, too, had grown more sophisticated. Prices for bear gallbladders had kept pace with increased demand in the Far East, where they are considered an aphrodisiac.

Many hunters equip their bear dogs with radio collars to make them easier to follow. The dogs frequently chase their quarry into the park, and, "of course the hunters'll always say their dogs got lost in the park," said Buchanan.

He told of finding one radio-collared dog that had been mauled by a bear. It was in the park where it shouldn't have been – and the collar "somehow" ended up on a wild boar. "One day the hunter'd think his dog was up near Cosby," he said. "The next it'd be way over in Greenbriar."

Buchanan and his friends also delighted in "getting" each other.

Acree told me about the time "someone" chained Buchanan's car to a tree while he was off in the woods – "and he couldn't track me because it was in gravel."

Asked about that story, Buchanan laughed and said, "Ask Bill Acree about the time he sat down on his Mace and then couldn't sit down at all for days."

And fellow tracker and FBI agent Bob Swabe had something to say about his forays into the woods with Buchanan and cohorts: "You always guard your backpack. Otherwise, before the day's over, you'll be carrying 15 or 20 pounds of rocks."

It was through tracking lost hikers and campers that Buchanan met Swabe. In 1986, that led to his being involved in one of the country's most extensive manhunts.

Swabe trained and handled dogs to follow scents.

"We worked on searches together: I didn't know about visual tracking, and he didn't know a damn thing about dogs," Swabe told me. "Tracking's sort of a lost art, and we felt like if we revived it, we could teach it to others."

With the FBI's Sterling Owen, Swabe developed a system for the office's SWAT team, designing a diamond pattern for following fugitives who might be armed.

"We wanted a formation that was safe yet effective," Owen explained. "The tracker, who is looking at the ground, is vulnerable, so we set this up to provide cover."

Essentially, the tracker moves with four SWAT team members, one in front, one in back and one on each wing.

In 1986, they put their method to work.

Michael Wayne Jackson, an Indiana parolee, had gone on a three-state killing spree before being flushed from a car near Wright City, Missouri, just west of St. Louis.

After he eluded a massive weeklong manhunt, the St. Louis FBI office called Knoxville and asked for Swabe and his dogs. Swabe suggested that Buchanan accompany them. "We had trained as a team," said Owen.

Surrounded by the SWAT team, Buchanan soon tracked the fugitive into a barn and to a ladder leading to the loft. As Swabe started climbing, there was a gunshot. The officers emptied the barn and cleared the area.

Several hours later, when they rushed the loft, they found that Jackson had committed suicide.

"I had to go up there and look to make sure it was the right one, the one I had been tracking," Buchanan said. "I was tracking tennis shoes – and it was the same one."

Along with a letter of commendation from then-FBI director William Webster, Buchanan's success against Jackson brought requests from across the country for classes in tracking. He then demonstrated his skills to law enforcement and search-and-rescue personnel from the high deserts of the Southwest to the low country of Georgia's coast.

He retired from the Park Service in 1989 and died, age 77, in 2004.

~~~~~~~~~~~

THE MOVE FROM 2303 West Clinch was the last I made before leaving Knoxville in 1972. In retrospect, the Tombo-in-the-tub incident made me realize, finally, that it was time to leave the university area, to close the Saloon for good.

When I made my decision, a Journal friend provided a perfect solution. Pat Fields, one of the area's best reporters and writers, lived in south Knoxville on Moody Avenue, only about five miles from downtown. She had just bought the house next door and offered it to me at a reasonable rent.

I enlisted friends – one had a pickup truck – and made the move. By that time my furnishings included, besides the jukebox, a wooden indoor telephone booth and a barber's chair. We saved those three items for the last trip.

One friend sat in the chair, white sheet around his neck and shaving cream on his face; another was in the phone booth, receiver to his ear; and a third acted like he was trying to select a record on the jukebox. We caused enough of a stir when we went through the campus that we circled around and made the trip again.

The house was two-bedroom, one full bath, with a studio-style addition over the attached garage that included a shower and a tiny kitchen. The room was perfect for my telephone booth and barber's chair. The main kitchen was spacious enough for the jukebox. I turned the other "kitchen" into a dark room for processing photo film.

The garage soon became home to a new addition to my vehicular inventory, a motorcycle.

On a late-summer day in 1970, not long after I had moved, I found myself trying to maneuver my dad's Ford station wagon along a sandy trail through the scrub outside of Gainesville, Florida. I was on the way to pick up a motorcycle, looking for a mobile home that I had been told was at the end of the trail.

The bike was a Yamaha 250 Big Bear; if I could find it and its owner, I was to transport it back to Knoxville for my friend Grady Amann.

It belonged to a man known to everyone as Peanut, a legend to motorcyclists around Knoxville. His reputation had been cemented when he participated in a Wall of Death attraction at the Tennessee Valley Fair a few years earlier. The Wall of Death stars bikers who go fast around a silo-shaped, wooden-floored track; the motorcycles and their riders are held up by friction and centrifugal force.

Stories of Peanut's Wall of Death skills had quickly spread through Lincoln Park, the north Knoxville neighborhood where he grew up, and by the fair's third day he was drawing big crowds. But his stint soon ended – the Wall's operators discovered that he was only 15 years old.

Knoxville police were also well aware of Peanut's riding skills. He was adept at off-roading through north-Knoxville neighborhoods with cops – limited to the streets – trying to pursue.

By the time of my trip to Florida, Peanut was in his mid-20s, and had moved to Florida several months after the demise of a partnership with Grady. The pair had pooled resources to buy a 1948 Aeronca Champ airplane, a purchase they made though neither knew how to fly. The deal died when Peanut crashed it while showing an official that he could land it. The Yamaha was to pay Grady for his half-interest in the Aeronca.

I found the mobile home and Peanut, loaded up the bike and eventually got it to Grady. A couple of months later, after getting hit by an un-seeing motorist on Atlantic Avenue, Grady worked out a deal with me: I traded him a set of drums for the now-banged-up Yamaha.

The Big Bear was designed for street travel, but by the time I acquired it I had become interested in motorcycle off-roading. A couple of friends and I turned the Yamaha into an incongruous dirt bike. Basically, I had next-to-nothing in it and saw its role as a vehicle for fun.

It had a registration tag, but it was expired, so riding on the street was always a risk. But there were occasions when I took the chance. Stanley and I hauled it to Nashville once. His parents, who had a swimming pool, lived there, but they frequently took weekend trips – when they were away we would take over the house, inviting Stanley's girlfriend and her sister, who lived in nearby Clarksville.

We were soon tooling through the fancy neighborhood of Belle Meade on the Yamaha, risking detection by police as we roared by the mansions of country-music stars.

But the most dangerous Yamaha escapades took place in Knoxville. There was one overcast Saturday night when I set out for a west Knoxville party on the bike. After I had gone a couple of miles it started raining. The downpour was heavy enough so that I was scared I was not going to make my destination. Fortunately I did, arriving soaking wet – and adding to a building wild-man reputation. I later talked a friend into giving me a ride home, leaving the Yamaha until I could get it the next afternoon after the rain had finally stopped.

But such trips were rare – mostly we stuck to off-road riding. Soon we were regulars at the dirt farm on top of Cherokee Bluff, a popular gathering spot for motorcyclists. Jumps had been built up, and there was plenty of space for playing around. We would load the Yamaha into the Scout and take it up to the Bluff.

The engine was two-cycle, which meant oil had to be added to each tank of gas. For that purpose, I carried an old Coca-Cola bottle, its 6.5-ounce capacity perfect for the task.

Eventually, the end of the gear-shift foot peg broke off. Replacements, I discovered, were not to be had. So we bent the rod out enough to get our foot under it to lift-shift it. Then the brake peg suffered the same fate – and the same fix. On the Bluff, the Yamaha, easily recognized because of its touring design (complete with full fenders and a bullet-shaped headlight) and its off-kilter front fork, was soon a star. The dirt-bikers couldn't believe we actually did some of the things we did on it. They didn't know we were attempting such tricks out of sheer ignorance.

Crashes in the dirt were, generally, no big deal – we weren't going fast enough to do much damage. And I had learned how to stay on top when I had to lay down the bike on my first day of ownership – forced to put it in a ditch beside Rutledge Pike when the car in front of me stopped suddenly.

Eventually, a friend and I decided to enter an enduro that was set up on wooded acreage at the foot of Chilhowee Mountain in Blount County. He not only had a dirt bike designed for such activity, but he also knew how to ride it.

We formed Paranoia Racing and paid our entry fees. Unfortunately, the Yamaha developed a problem with the throttle cable – it started sticking. Riding it became decidedly dangerous. So I had to scratch. The other half of our team made the race but failed to finish, though he did limp back to our vehicle covered in enough mud to look like a veteran motorcycle racer.

I never solved the sticking cable and, after nearly breaking my neck kicking it off on a hill near my Moody Avenue house, sold it for $50, my dream of a Wall of Death appearance at an end.

~~~~~~~~~~~

BY THE TIME of the move to Moody, the Vietnam War had been at full-tilt for several years, a fearful alternative for anyone of draft age. For many of us, it had been sufficient to insure college-class attendance.

Since UT was a federal land-grant school, two years of Reserve Officer Training Corps was a requirement for male students, with Advanced ROTC an option for anyone interested in pursuing the military. Because of high blood pressure, I ended up being exempt from ROTC (and, after graduation, from the military altogether.) A couple of my high school friends, who didn't see continued schooling as an option, enlisted in the military right out of high school. One, the older brother of one of my best friends, was East High's first Vietnam casualty, honored with a posthumous Silver Star for heroism. Today, Burlington's Donald A. Sherrod library building is named for him.

The Journal, which functioned as the state Republican Party's house organ, was a staunch backer of the U.S. involvement in Vietnam. Editor Guy Smith had served as a national party leader, and his successor, Bill Childress, followed his example: the Journal was a partisan publication, and it was unabashedly conservative. But most of the younger staffers were liberal and anti-war.

Though the war began to dominate the news, it didn't always get top play in the Journal, especially during an election season. An endorsement for a Journal favorite like Sen. Howard Baker Jr. might dominate Page One in spite of what was happening in the rest of the world. One journalistic embarrassment involved the start of the Six-Day War in the Mideast. The Journal limited the story to four paragraphs and played it inside the paper.

But as the war in southeast Asia progressed, it frequently topped the page. In fact, the headline writers joked that we should keep a banner on standby: "B-52s Pound Supply Routes." That much was certain on a daily basis.

But, despite the macabre jokes, area war fatalities always received strong coverage. And, eventually, as protests spread to Knoxville and the UT campus, the Journal couldn't ignore the anti-war movement.

One of the first gatherings that the city editor decided was worthy of the Journal's time wasn't quite important enough to send a veteran newsman. One of the greener college students was dispatched. Unfortunately, the reporter chosen, unlike most of his cohorts, was naïve about what was going on in the country.

His story made him the object of newsroom ridicule for days. He referred to the African-American attendees holding up their fists and shouting "Right Arm" after exhortations by the speakers. Fortunately, the city editor caught the mistake and changed it to "Right On." He escaped embarrassment in print, but for days the rest of us greeted him with a raised fist and "Right Arm."

I was working as an editor at the time, so my newsroom duties kept me inside and away from what was happening on campus. I did manage to attend a speech by the antiwar activist William Kunstler in Circle Park that took place while I was off from work. The crowd seemed to be about equally divided between anti-war activists and police.

The speech received nominal coverage with the emphasis on the outrage it brought from local politicians – typical of the ineptness of Knoxville media, the Journal included.

It took a visit from President Richard Nixon, through the auspices of his friend, evangelist Billy Graham, to get Knoxville's attention. And it took the national media to provide comprehensive – and insightful – coverage.

Gary Wills's story for Esquire magazine carried the headline "How Nixon Used the Media, Billy Graham, and the Good Lord to Rap with Students at Tennessee U." That was followed by a memorable sub-head: "Jesus wept."

The accompanying picture by Don Dudenbostel, photographer for the student newspaper, The Daily Beacon, depicted an African-American student hiding in front of helmeted riot police in the shrubbery in front of Ayres Hall. He was looking at the camera and holding up two fingers in the universal "peace" sign. The photo became one of the era's iconic images.

Graham's week-long crusade took place in May 1970 in Neyland Stadium and drew people from all over the area. Nixon came in on Thursday the 28th, accompanied by Henry

Kissinger and H.R. Haldeman among others from his staff. The national media was also present – until Nixon had ended his brief talk, when they quickly moved to the media room in the bowels of the stadium to file their stories.

A friend, Jim Stovall, a senior journalism major, was working as a reporter at the News-Sentinel and had already completed his work for the night, so he joined them out of curiosity.

"I was watching all these national figures at their typewriters and phones when someone grabbed my arm from behind," he remembers. "I turned around and it was Helen Thomas, the long-time UPI White House correspondent. She was on the phone dictating and impatiently asked me how far the demonstrators were from the stage where Nixon was. I told her 30 yards – easy enough because it was a football field and the anti-Nixon people were set up on the 30-yard line and the stage was in the end zone."

A star White House reporter couldn't be expected to know the measurements of a football field.

~~~~~~~~~~

THOUGH I HAD graduated UT a couple of years earlier, I had stayed on at the Journal because of a couple of promotions and raises. I was being paid a living wage, had Fridays and Saturdays off and work, for the most part, was still fun.

Since the Journal was a morning newspaper, the staffers who actually produced the stories worked at night. And most of the brass left at 5 p.m. That meant that newsroom antics could get crazy as the night wore on.

Several of the veterans were as likely to be drunk by 9 p.m. as not; the student staffers often had joined them in sharing bottles or had snuck off to smoke marijuana. The newspaper library – the morgue – had its own door and was unstaffed after 5 p.m. It was the site of hidden half-pints, and, occasionally, the passing around of joints.

One night, there was a newsroom fire, an incident that has been passed down over the decades as part of Knoxville newspaper lore. The episode began with a prank and ended with ax-wielding firemen running up the stairs and bursting into the second-floor newsroom.

Involved were several copy editors, the news editor, the political reporter, and, most prominently, the city-hall reporter.

The result included scorched ceiling tiles, half-burned stories destined to run in the paper that were now thoroughly drenched by the contents of a fire extinguisher, an empty gallon rubber-cement can, and a half-soaked political reporter. And, after the fire department's departure, an embarrassed telephone call as the news editor attempted to explain to the managing editor why his paper was going to be late.

The veterans included city-hall reporter Ron McMahan, notorious for keeping a desk overrun with newspapers, clippings, wadded carbon paper, Blue Circle bags and shriveled fries left from weeks-old meals, an ashtray full of cigarette butts, and other unidentifiable bits of detritus.

McMahan's office domain was next to the horseshoe-shaped copy desk, the hub of the newsroom, which was peopled primarily by grizzled veterans.

The news editor sat in the slot of the copy desk with six editors seated around the outside edge. The wire editor, Bob Adams, occupied the seat at the end closest to the room where the Associated Press machines clattered out the latest world developments.

The copy editors and some of the reporters periodically admonished McMahan to clean up his desk, pointing out that the cockroaches housed in the empty hamburger bags were widening their food-search circles to include the neighboring work stations.

Most of the time, McMahan ignored his neighbors' comments, but a couple of times a year the mess would become unbearable even to him. He would then delegate a copy clerk to clean up his desk. "Throw away everything except the clippings," he would say.

The fire episode followed one such tidy-up. As McMahan beamed at his newly cleaned desk, he compared it to the mess of the copy desk, covered with typed-up stories for the next issue and ripped-up newspaper pages and pica poles and glue pots.

Then he went to dinner. And the copy editors went to work.

Within minutes McMahan's desk was trashed: wadded up newspaper pages, carbon paper, rubber cement puddles decorated with shavings from pencil sharpeners and the contents of ash trays. The copy clerk who had cleaned the desk tried to stop the desecration but finally fled to the Blue Circle up the street, wisely deciding to take a dinner hour of his own.

When McMahan returned, he took one look at his desk and walked back to the storage closet, returning with a one-gallon can of rubber cement. He uncapped the can, climbed on top of the copy desk and walked around it pouring rubber cement over everything, including wire photos and stories for the upcoming Four Star edition.

Just as McMahan jumped down, Adams emerged from the wire room and saw the glint of the rubber cement on the desk in front of his chair. And someone said, "Whatever you do, Bob, don't strike a match."

Naturally, that's what he did.

The glue went all-around the horseshoe and, in an instant, so did the flames.

As everyone jumped back, one staffer had the presence to phone the fire department, and another grabbed the fire extinguisher from the wall and started working on the flames. Political reporter Ralph Griffith, seeing humor in the situation, began laughing in his annoying high-pitched cackle. He, too, was hosed with the extinguisher.

By the time the firemen arrived, the flames were out and the copy desk crew was trying to salvage what they could of the Four Star stories and photos.

And the slot man, news editor Byron Drinnon, was busy on the phone explaining to managing editor Steve Humphrey why his hand-delivered copy of the Four Star was going to be late.

In normal times, when Drinnon left about 9 p.m. the newsroom lost its only remaining sober – and/or adult – staffer, and the copy desk became the bull-shooting center, with the late sports-department people and the night police reporter frequently joining in. Veterans re-told old tales for the benefit of rookies, gossip was swapped about the brass, and plots were hatched.

Sometimes outsiders would wander in – the door onto Clinch Avenue stayed open until 2 a.m. The Blue Circle on the corner, the Krystal a half-block away on Gay Street and the two pool rooms above it, were open even later.

Girlfriends often would join the crew, sometimes bringing six-packs or other supplies.

One night, a plot was hatched involving the newspaper's "society" section, which was produced by three women, all of whom were "of" the milieu. Their work domain was a separate office, befitting their status and, probably, to shield them from the raucous activity of the newsroom. The three finished their workday at 5 p.m., just when the rest of the newsroom was beginning its deadline runs. The lights of their office would be turned off, the door shut, the office a quiet refuge in a noisy, profane world.

So it was the place of choice for those who needed peace and quiet – to make a personal phone call, to sleep off a nasty hangover, to pass out from a long, whiskey-fueled day.

It was also clean and neat, something that most of the newsroom was not. The Society ladies kept their desks clear of everything except a telephone and in-and-out baskets. A person in need of rest had only to carefully move a couple of items to have space for an aching head.

During my tenure at the Journal, more than once a rim-rat (as copy-desk denizens were known), who had gone missing would be found asleep in Society.

The department was womaned by two long-time employees and a third younger helper. The third person would be someone just out of Smith or Vassar or Sweet Briar, needing work experience until a suitable husband-to-be was snared.

Sometimes the third person, still impressionable, would be drawn to the newsroom antics and would linger at the desk of one of the reporters, entranced by a lurid tale of crime from a police reporter or an unprintable story of moral degeneracy from the political realm. The latter might even involve someone widely known in her circle.

Most of the rim-rats, gracious though they might be to the Society ladies in person, made fun of them when it was time to proof-read their pages.

One night, as a weekly feature involving a recipe sent in by a reader was being proofed, a theory was born: The Society ladies did not pay attention to the recipes. A plot was concocted. What if a bogus recipe, a recipe for an outrageous dish, was mailed in – would Society recognize it as a prank?

To test our theory, Carp Surprise was created. Carp is a bottom-feeding fish that is seldom eaten, but, for our experiment, we imagined it stuffed with a spinach mixture, a mixture spiced with nutmeg and sweetened with just a touch of sorghum. There were other ingredients in the stuffing as well, ingredients selected to make an unpalatable fish even more sickening. Suitably stuffed, the fish would then be baked to a golden hue.

A reader was invented, given a bogus Sequoyah Hills address, and the recipe was typed up and mailed to the Journal, attention of the Reader's Recipes editor.

The Society ladies, ignorant of bottom-feeders in general, had, within a couple of weeks, edited our Carp Surprise entry, headlined it and sent it to the composing room to be set into type. (The printers charged with handling the copy had been tipped off to our plot.) Our theory was proven. Now, if our concoction could just make the newspaper.

But it was not to be. Unfortunately, the managing editor, by sheer chance, happened to see the page proof. A former outdoors editor and a long-time fisherman, he immediately detected the odor of a rat – a rim-rat.

There was a quick phone call to the Society editor and our creation was tossed.

The Society office was the breeding ground for other late-night pranks, too. Initiation tradition for new reporters involved a phony, called-in obituary or story, which could be phoned in to the neophyte from one of the desks in Society. Such efforts were not intended for publication – the victim would be laughed at and his notes thrown away.

One of the more memorable involved a Hawkins County farmer whose named survivors included Furry, his pet squirrel. In another, a new sports clerk was given information on a Claiborne County football game that involved a touchdown that was worth only one point "because it was from the one-yard line."

And the office refuge had other uses, too, especially after-midnight when girlfriends would visit. A dark room, a door that closed – to employ that hoary Society-section cliche', a good time was had by all.

~~~~~~~~~~

SOON AFTER I started work at the Journal, I was introduced to a game called Far-Away. It was simple, easily played during work and involved absolutely no skill. The buy-in was $2, plus the price of a six-and-a-half ounce bottle of Coca-Cola from the vending machine in the composing room. The Cokes, as I recall, were a quarter.

The re-fillable bottles had the name of the city where they originated embossed on the bottom. Newer bottles did not have the city's name – they were blank.

The object was to get the bottle that was from farthest away. A Knoxville bottle was a sure loser, Del Rio, Texas, a strong contender. If a prospective player argued that the game was pure gamble without any redeeming value, a veteran would point out that players were getting an education in geography. Disagreements would lead to the large U.S. map on the wall of the newsroom and a tape measure kept solely for such disputes.

Del Rio was almost always a winner, beating Bay City, Michigan by a few miles. Douglas, Arizona was only beatable by the rare Los Angeles or by a blank, which was an automatic winner.

Far-Away was not the only gambling in the workplace. During football season, parlay sheets were common. And there was always a punch-board or two being run by printers. Usually the payoff was a bottle of whiskey, but occasionally a hunting rifle or a shotgun would be the prize. I won a deer rifle once, fired it a few times to see how it worked, then ran it off myself on a punch board.

Other firearms figured into an episode involving a more serious gambler, an occasional late-night visitor to the newsroom. He was known by a nickname and frequented Comer's pool room. He also ran his own betting book. I'll call him Slim here.

Slim was a loud-mouth, cocksure that he knew everything concerning sports and odds and handicapping. He could be a problem, especially when he had been drinking, and that frequently led to his being thrown out of Comer's. When that happened he would sometimes wander into the Journal sports department where the Associated Press wire machine would be clattering with the latest scores.

The last time I saw Slim had nothing to do with late-night scores, but everything to do with alcohol and his cock-sure attitude.

After leaving work at 2 a.m., a cohort and I had stopped in the Krystal on the Strip. Fred was working night police and I was the late news editor and we wanted an early breakfast. We were seated at the front-window counter so as not to miss anything interesting along Cumberland Avenue when I saw, reflected in the glass, Slim coming in the door. He was wearing a trench coat.

I nudged my companion; we didn't turn around, hoping he wouldn't notice us. Unfortunately, he did. After getting a cup of coffee, Slim came over to tell us how well he was doing with his book, how nobody could best him when it came to sports betting, how nobody at Comer's knew anything. He was obviously drunk.

Then a police car pulled into the parking lot, its occupant exiting to get his own cup of coffee. Slim took no notice, continuing to loudly regale us with his boasting. Finally, as the cop approached the door, I warned Slim to cool it, that a policeman was coming in. Without turning around, he pulled two revolvers from his trench-coat pockets, one in each hand.

"I'm not scared of him," he announced.

As Fred and I quickly moved away, Slim laughed and put the guns back in his pockets. By then, we were going out the door, headed to my car, keeping an eye on Slim. When I pulled onto Cumberland, Slim was coming out the door, too, nonchalantly headed to his car.

"The cop never even noticed him," Fred said. "I guess the odds were with Slim tonight." And us, too, I didn't need to add.

~~~~~~~~~~

THOUGH OUR ENCOUNTER with Slim had taken place at the Krystal, we were usually more picky when choosing our late-night eats.

The Krystal was reliable, but we often opted for something that was, shall we say, more exotic. And we could always count on Grady Amann, who seemed to be a regular at every dark-of-night hangout in Knox County. When the time came – 2 a.m. – he would stop by my spot on the copy desk with a, "Wanna scoff some grease?"

His usual query notwithstanding, Grady was discerning when it came to food, whether it was fresh-picked corn "found" in a field in south Knox County, chili slaw dogs at Dis & Dat on Chapman Highway or barbecue from Brother Jack's.

Brother Jack's was in a sketchy part of town, close enough to the UT campus that it became a must-visit for students in the late 1960s.

Jack specialized in barbecue – or more accurately, food products made from pig parts. There were smoked ribs and pulled pork, to be sure, but also on offer were pig burgers, hand-made ground-pork patties between two slices of white bread. The sandwiches or meals were served in Styrofoam containers. They could be had with chips and a cold soft drink. And hot sauce.

When Jack, a large black man, took your order, he would smile and say, "You want that hot, don't you?" And then he would sauce it from a squeeze bottle, the contents his own recipe. And it was capital-H hot.

But the limited menu was not the only distinguishing aspect of Brother Jack's. First, there was no sign telling the seeker that he had found it; second, the food was to-go only; and third, the place was open late, usually until 3 a.m. or so.

Brother Jack's was on University Avenue, only about a mile from Fort Sanders and its population of UT students – on the wrong side of the interstate. Just as getting drunk on prodigious amounts of beer at the Roman Room was a rite of passage, so were experiences at Brother Jack's.

One popular stunt was taking a sorority-girl date to Brother Jack's after a big dance, then cautioning her about getting the sauce on her gown as you drove back to campus with pig burgers.

In "Real Barbecue," the definitive guidebook authored by Vince Staten and Greg Johnson, Staten recalls driving one date to Brother Jack's and telling her to wait while he went inside to get a couple of sandwiches. She insisted that he give her the car keys – "I'll come back and pick you up in 10 minutes," she said. "I'm not going to sit here, even with the car doors locked."

When Staten and I visited the place in the early 1980s during research for the book, it was the only time either of us had stopped there in daylight.

Sometimes during our college days, if we were feeling particularly devious, we would tease dates by telling them that they had just had a real treat – barbecued possum.

I had picked up possum lore at an early age. When I was about 10, my friends and I spotted a furry animal up a persimmon tree in a wooded lot near my house. Someone in the group recognized it as a possum and said we should "shake" it down.

Our possum-savvy companion then climbed the tree to get to the limb where the animal was clinging and started shaking. When the animal hit the ground, it appeared to be dead. And I learned the origin of the term "playing possum." On a dare, I picked the possum up by the tail, and it quickly curled back and tried to take a bite out of my hand.

Eventually, we managed to get it back to my house, where my dad was working in the yard.

"He's not hurt," he informed us. "Don't put him down." Then he got a cardboard box and we placed the possum inside. "Come on," Dad said and we climbed into the station wagon, carefully placing the boxed possum in the back.

Three miles later, we stopped at the house of a black man my dad knew. "He'll want it," he said. The possum was transferred to its new owner, who then informed us that after it was fattened up it would make a fine meal.

On the trip back, Dad told us how the animal would be caged, then fed persimmons and table scraps until it was "eatin' size." Possum fattened on corn-bread, he added, was particularly tasty.

I never took the stories of Brother Jack's serving possum seriously – until years later when Grady told me about an experience he had with Brother Jack.

"When me and Danny West and Herschel Peek went over there one night," he said, "Jack told us he wanted to show us something and motioned us behind the counter to his stove. There in a big roasting pan was a large animal cooking on low heat. The head was still on it. We thought that the rumors were true. So I said, 'That's a big possum, Brother Jack.'

"He chuckled and said, 'That's no possum, that's much better. That's a raccoon'. But it ain't ready yet – I'll save you some if you want to come back tomorrow'."

"We laughed," Grady said, "and told him we'd stick to rib sandwiches and pig burgers.

"Of course," Grady added with a grin, "Who knows what kind of meat he used to make the patties for the pig burgers? Maybe we've been eating possum and raccoon all along."

Preparing for Departure

A Sixties' soundtrack – Streaking and tragedy on the Strip – Streetcar, Speedy and other drunks – Sexcapades with the Duffer – The script girl and a missed opportunity – Cockfighting "banty roosters" – Union organizing – Setting the stage for the next chapter

~~~~~~~~~~

THE CAMPUS business district – the Strip – morphed over the decades from a mix of four-plex apartment buildings and small businesses to single-residence houses turned into bars. Today it's a mix of chain fast-food establishments and bars.

In the early 1960s, the grandmother of one of my high school friends ran a boarding house in the 1800 block of Cumberland Avenue. Next door was a bar that changed into a music venue on weekend nights, much to her consternation. She warned us never to venture in that direction.

But by the time I started attending UT in 1963, the Strip was changing – not surprising as UT enrollment jumped from 13,000 to 25,000 in less than five years. And, of course, the national mood was changing with the acceleration of civil-rights activism, feminism and protest against the war in Vietnam.

The protests were led by the young, and as rock 'n' roll's sense of fun was melded with folk music's social agenda, music was providing the soundtrack. On the Strip, that meant nightclubs that had been featuring beach music for the shag-dancers were now following what was being played on the radio, what was being recorded. And that was quite a mix, from Bob Dylan to the Rolling Stones to Marvin Gaye to Peter, Paul and Mary, from drug paeans to anti-war anthems.

It was a high-stakes era and, thanks to widespread access to radio and television, everyone could tune in.

Those freewheeling years, from the mid-1960s to the mid-1970s, became the Strip's defining decade.

A walk down Cumberland Avenue meant the heady aroma of incense, encounters with hippies seeking spare change, opportunities to acquire weed or hash or acid.

Music by Cream or Jimi Hendrix or Mott the Hoople or Marvin Gaye blared from stores and record shops. Or a radio station might be running a "remote" from one of the head shops.

For the most part, radio disc jockeys played what they wanted, the music that they liked, the music that they knew their listeners wanted to hear. The patter, too, was open, sometimes pushing against the boundaries of "good taste," whatever that meant.

One of the more popular radio personalities was Eddie Beacon. I met Beacon when he started dating a girl I knew through one of my Journal friends. Steve Horne lived in an apartment in Fort Sanders, the basement of a large house that had been split into three different residences, one to each floor. The middle was occupied by four female students, the top by a radio part-timer – student sometimes, late-night disc jockey full-time. Beacon was one of his friends; he met the girl (I'll call her Susie here) who lived downstairs and they started going out.

Eventually, after Knoxville's radio playlists started becoming more rigid, more business-oriented, Beacon, Susie and friends loaded a station wagon and moved to Los Angeles. I lost touch.

Several years after I had returned to Knoxville in the late 1990s, I heard that Beacon was in Knoxville and still working in radio. A retrospective look at the Strip and its music seemed to be in order, so I managed to get a group of Strip stalwarts together for a story for the weekly alternative publication, The Knoxville Mercury.

Through the mid '60s, the dominant Top 40 music station in the Knoxville area had been WNOX, which had studios in north Knoxville and boasted a clear-channel 50,000-watt signal. The airwave changes that were coming began there.

John Pirkle was part of the WNOX lineup at that time, as was Beacon, just beginning his radio career. Beacon began as the overnight DJ and soon became popular as "your Swingin' Deacon."

As the music changed and radio began experimenting with formats, WNOX began playing album cuts during the overnight segment, midnight to 6 a.m. Beacon worked that shift from the transmission tower in north Knoxville – "babysitting the transmitter," as he says.

"Beacon started as our all-night guy," Pirkle recalls, adding with a laugh that, "the dregs of society would be out doing a night run, and they'd find Beacon."

I don't know if I fit that description, but once I had been promoted to state-desk reporter at the Journal, I didn't get off work until 11:30 p.m. (later 2 a.m.), and Beacon provided my soundtrack for a couple of hours every night.

Thanks to the Swingin' Deacon, I first heard such acts as Mott the Hoople, the Kinks, Traffic, Cream, and Jimi Hendrix.

Sometimes Beacon had company at his late-night post, a small concrete-block building isolated in a field. It was, he said, "a party waiting to happen." When your voice and the music you like is being broadcast over the air, you may be alone, but you're not exactly isolated, he added. One night, he was joined by some of his station cohorts. The result was that he experienced his first serious confrontation with management and his first firing – from the station that had given him his first chance on the air.

"A couple of other DJs showed up, hammered," Beacon says. "They'd been to a concert. They wanted me to go get some more beer, and they took over the broadcast. When I came back they were doing a parody of a golf commentary, using the real names of personalities from another station. After they heard about it, they were ready to sue for slander. Part of the settlement was that all three of us were fired."

So in 1969, Beacon began a new job at WKGN, which had studios in the 2200 block of the Strip in space now occupied by the Sunspot restaurant.

"I was on 10 p.m. to midnight, playing pretty much what I wanted to, album cuts," he says. "A lot of the Allman Brothers, Wet Willie, Procol Harem, Cream. The switchboard would light up with calls from UT students.

"I had all my albums stacked on the floor. Then one day I came in at 7 p.m. and they were all gone. I asked where they were and I was told that [the station owner] didn't like that music and didn't want it played anymore. That was it. So I went back to my car and drove off."

Once again, the Swingin' Deacon was without a pulpit. So he and friends departed for Los Angeles.

As Beacon's story demonstrates, what was being played and what management favored wasn't always the same. But that changed, at least for one Knoxville station, when Pirkle took over as station manager of WROL.

"The owner wanted to build up the station and sell it," Pirkle says. "I had gotten a license to start my own station and was in the process of building it when he came to me and asked if I could do what he wanted with his station.

"Dick Sterchi [another veteran of Knoxville radio] and I had worked together before and we agreed to take it over. Dick took care of the business side, and I took care of the on-air part."

Pirkle moved the tower to a hill in northwest Knoxville so he could target his signal to the UT campus. Though the station was officially still WROL, he changed the on-air handle to W149 (the station was on the dial at 1490), and the DJs began playing album cuts. What had been a late-night-only format was now standard, at least for one station.

The phone lines lit up, and the station "outkicked its signal" in the ratings, Pirkle said. (The station's signal was one of the weaker ones in the market – but because of the tower's location, it was strong around UT.)

Knoxville's counter-culture, me included, now had a radio station playing the music we wanted to hear all the time – with like-minded DJs adding kick-ass commentary.
The album format meant longer cuts with the DJs frequently playing songs that might push 10 minutes in length.

"You would keep the longer cuts like 'Stairway to Heaven' handy for when you needed a bathroom break," remembers Gary Adkins, who DJed at W149 and later at Q15, another station that had begun following Pirkle's format model. "I became conditioned," he says, claiming with a laugh that even today when he hears Lynyrd Skynyrd's "Free Bird" he has to go to the bathroom.

Another of Pirkle's early moves was calling Beacon in Los Angeles. The Swingin' Deacon returned to Knoxville and again became the late-night DJ that everybody around campus was listening to.

Soon, there were other radio personalities being heard and talked about. Besides Beacon, Pirkle's lineup included Rob

"Monkey Monkey" Galbraith, known for sly hillbilly-tinged humor, and the always irreverent Bill Johnson.

And there were Adkins and Alan Sneed, tagged The Brothers, and always pushing the limits with their patter.

Adkins adds that there was a late-night DJ on for a period called Motorhead. "He played nothing but Frank Zappa. He'd come in with a ball of hash and play Zappa and smoke all night. The morning news guy would come in and complain about the studio smelling like pot."

There was another overnight DJ who liked to play music by an English space-rock group called Hawkwind. "He'd play both sides of the album straight through," Adkins says.

Management, obviously, wasn't around for the overnight shift.

Live remotes, still a fixture of radio, were also popular with businesses on the Strip. Johnson recalls one at a head shop that featured Miss Nude USA. "She was sitting in a papasan chair in the front window, buck naked with all these college boys outside. She was there for four hours."

Beacon once did a remote from an Alcoa Highway strip joint. "When you're doing a remote, you talk with the owner, or the salesmen, about the business. What could I talk about at a strip club? That was a long shift."

There were also appearances by artists promoting concerts or new records. Adkins remembers one in particular.

"Greg Allman came into the studio with Sweet William (Bill Sauls, a local singer who fronted the Stereos and sometimes went on the road with the Allman Brothers). People were calling, and Greg announces that he's going to sit in with Sauls that night at the Casual Lounge on Central. There was a huge traffic jam, and the place was packed. They played until 3 a.m."

Studio interviews with name acts were common. "We interviewed a who's who of rock 'n' roll," says Johnson. "Alice Cooper, Manfred Mann, Nazareth, Lynyrd Skynyrd."

Those acts were in town playing the clubs. Manfred Mann did a gig at Bradley's Station on Cumberland, Frankie Valli and the Four Seasons, with Rufus Thomas opening, headlined at The Place, a longtime fixture on the Strip.

"One of the fans invited Frankie and the band to her house in south Knoxville after the show and they all went, Rufus included," says Chip Emerson, who was a part-owner of The Place. The party went on all night.

The Place was also the site of an early Jimmy Buffett show, set up by Pirkle, who by then was partners with club-owner Kenneth Kelly in Concept 90, a concert-promotion, band-management company.

My roommate at the time was working for Concept 90, and we ended up hanging out with Buffett and his crew after the show. We made it home just as the sun was coming up.

Then, as now, venues along the Strip came and went, victims of liquor-license revocations, ownership changes and fickle tastes.

There was Foxy Lady, Friday's Child, the Twin Light, the Pump Room, the Orange Peel, Sound Showcase, Bradley's Station.

Popular local bands included the Loved Ones, the Plebeians, Southern Cross, Cowcatcher, and Fatback, which later became one of Knoxville's music success stories as the Amazing Rhythm Aces.

After touring with Canadian Jesse Winchester, with lead singer and songwriter Russell Smith fronting, the Aces produced several chart-topping albums. Their singles "Third Rate Romance," "Amazing Grace (Used to Be Her Favorite Song)" and "The End Is Not in Sight" were major hits, with the latter winning a Grammy in 1976.

The free-wheeling playlist atmosphere helped fuel the always fierce radio competition, and promotions and remote stunts accelerated. Management at W149 bought a de-commissioned fire truck and frequently used it, bell clanging.

"I had to drive that thing," Beacon remembers. "And it wasn't easy to drive."

Later, after he had moved over to 15Q, management came up with the idea of a "15Q Millionaire," and Beacon again got the call.

"They put me in a tuxedo and a top hat, and I was supposed to be giving all this money away. And they're driving me around in a Gremlin [a small car produced by the now-defunct American Motors Company]. I'd go into a grocery store and pick out someone with a cart full of groceries and pay for it all."

The stunt culminated in a turn on the Ferris Wheel at the Tennessee Valley Fair in Chilhowee Park.

"I had a garbage bag full of dollar bills and dumped them out from my seat up in the air, and they floated everywhere. All these people were grabbing and pushing, and of course some kid got hurt and there was a lawsuit."

Eventually, as the music changed, as the Sixties sputtered out and disco took over pop culture's soundtrack, there was a move toward corporate consolidation of radio and rigid playlists for DJs to follow. Nowadays, radio is known for its talk formats more than for music.

The free-wheeling days came to an end. But the kids who were part of the Strip's Sixties scene, who return to the Strip for football game days or to give their families a tour of the old stomping grounds, recall that era with fondness.

"It was music, mirth and merriment," says Johnson.

"Wild-west time," Emerson adds with a chuckle.

"An awful lot of people remember, and it's primarily because of the music," says Beacon.

That is certainly true for me. One of the songs that I was introduced to by Beacon's show was from a legendary English rocker named Long John Baldry. It's called "Don't Try to Lay No Boogie-Woogie on the King of Rock 'n' Roll" and, with its spoken introduction clocks at almost seven minutes. It's on my iPhone and gets played at least once a week, more than 50 years after I first heard it.

~~~~~~~~~~~

EVEN AFTER I HAD moved from Knoxville, visits back home usually included hanging out on the Strip with friends. One Saturday night during the mid-1970s, I was back in town on a weekend when the streaking fad – running naked in public – made it to the Strip. With the crowds bringing Cumberland Avenue traffic to a standstill and the police trying to restore order, my friends and I watched as an audacious kid raised the bar for the other streakers: he ran naked up and over the top of a police cruiser. He then disappeared into the crowd before the cop could exit his car and nab him.

Cumberland Avenue is more than the business and entertainment district for the university. It is also two U.S. highways, 11 and 70. Until Interstate 40 was completed, that meant the thoroughfare was the main route for east-west truck traffic. And that meant frequent traffic snarls.

Even after the interstate was opened in the early 1960s, it was only four lanes initially, and a heavy snowfall usually meant traffic trouble. The truckers, familiar with Cumberland from previous trips, would sometimes switch to the parallel thoroughfare. And when UT classes had been canceled because of the weather, students would gather on the Strip.

Cumberland Avenue's long ascent east from the railroad overpass meant there was sledding – if snow and ice halted traffic. When conditions were right, students brought out sleds and large pieces of cardboard – even the occasional pair of skis – and used Cumberland Avenue as their Green Diamond slope. For a lift back to the top at 19th Street, they could hitch rides by hanging onto the back bumpers of tractor-trailer trucks slowly working their way up the hill.

After one heavy snowfall, a group of friends and I equipped an aluminum john boat with a rocking chair and used it as an unwieldy sled, forcing skiers and sledders to dodge us as we tried to maneuver.

The snow-day incidents came to an end, at least for several years, after an incident involving snowballs and a tractor-trailer truck resulted in tragedy. A student was killed, and UT stopped cancelling classes during snowstorms.

The snowfall that day began early, and by mid-day students were adding to the jams on Cumberland, snowballing each other and the occasional vehicle slipping and sliding as drivers attempted to climb the hill.

A tractor-trailer became stalled in the middle of the intersection at 19th Street and was pelted. The driver panicked, pulled out a pistol and fired into the crowd, fatally hitting a student. The crowd surrounded the trucker, disarming him and pulling him from his cab. The bouncer of The Pump Room (a nightclub on the southwest corner of the intersection) rescued him from the students and held him until police arrived.

The victim was from New Jersey, attending UT because he had relatives on the faculty. His aunt had been my English teacher one quarter. At his trial, the truck driver confessed that he was high on amphetamines and was convicted of manslaughter. He served several years in prison. Until the early 2000s, the university maintained a policy that classes would continue despite heavy snowfall.

~~~~~~~~~~

EVEN AFTER MY move from Fort Sanders, I still had friends living there and it was still the center of our nightlife. And, though I had curtailed my partying, I was still meeting friends for a beer at Brownie's or the Quarterback, or if it was after midnight and we were hungry, we would go to the open-24-hours Krystal.

And the Journal was still providing eye-opening reminders that it was time for me to get serious about my future. One such was a veteran reporter who was known all over town by his nickname, Speedy.

The nickname was bestowed when he was a star running back at a local high school. He was quick and accomplished enough to receive a football scholarship to UT. The way Speedy told it, as a freshman he quickly distinguished himself by winning a rookie-initiation ritual involving drinking large amounts of beer.

He left UT for the Army, serving in the Korean conflict. Eventually, after returning to UT and graduating, Speedy was hired by the Journal.

Speedy was an excellent reporter – thanks to his football heroics, he had a lot of contacts around town. But he also was a heavy drinker, which led to his divorce and his dismissal from the newspaper more than once. The last time he was fired came on a Friday afternoon, when he was arrested for public drunkenness a hundred yards or so from the office. At the time he was working night police, 5 p.m. to 2 a.m., a position he had been given when he was hired back following his previous firing.

After parking his car on the Church Avenue viaduct, Speedy started across the street for the newspaper building. A policeman noticed his wobbling and stopped him. When the cop asked if he was drunk, we learned later, Speedy argued that he couldn't be drunk because he was on his way to work. A couple of the paper's engravers saw the arrest and told the city editor; Speedy was fired again.

When I first started work at the Journal as a copy boy, I occupied the space immediately in front of his desk, a position that meant I was privy to his insights about his fellow reporters and, more importantly, the bosses. I quickly learned that he was smart and possessed a rapier-like wit.

One of his fellow reporters was known to everyone as the laziest person in the newsroom – treating story deadlines as mere suggestions. Speedy referred to him as Chained Lightning, a sarcastic moniker that was soon taken up by everyone else. (Chained Lightning eventually found a job more suited to his skills and left the Journal to become an editor for a weekly newspaper, where he had only one deadline every seven days).

Unfortunately, Speedy's periods of sobriety became shorter and shorter – he was fired from the Journal three times during the seven years I worked there. After taking the cure, he would be re-hired because of his skills and his contacts.

Speedy was not the only newsroom employee who had a problem with alcohol. Some I had first-hand dealings with; others, whose tenure had taken place long before I was hired, I only heard about because of their stunts.

One of the latter, whose nickname was Streetcar, once flustered a new church reporter while he was involved in a face-to-face interview in the newsroom with a prominent Knoxville preacher. Slipping up behind the reporter, Streetcar gently kissed him on the head. The preacher then tried to listen to the embarrassed reporter's explanation without joining the laughter from nearby staffers.

Streetcar's last dismissal came after he disappeared while working on a story in Cocke County, northeast of Knoxville. He and a photographer were sent to the county seat, Newport, for interviews. At some point, the photographer explained when he got back to Knoxville, Streetcar had stopped at a bootlegger's to get a drink. After waiting in vain at their agreed-on rendezvous point, the photographer drove back to Knoxville. Streetcar finally showed up at the office several days later to find that his desk had been cleaned out.

Decades later, when I was living and working in Atlanta, I became friends with the writer Paul Hemphill, who was also a veteran of newspapers – and of heavy drinking. Hemphill had long since given up alcohol, but he remembered his time hanging out with Streetcar. When he heard I was from

Knoxville, he immediately asked if I had known him. Though he had been dead for years, it seems Streetcar was a legend in Atlanta as well as in Knoxville. He had, I learned from Hemphill, been fired from several newspapers around the south. He died in obscurity, a not-quite-forgotten drunk, at a relatively young age.

Another hard-drinking former Knoxville newsman, a frequent Journal newsroom habitué though he worked in radio, later fashioned an illustrious career in sports broadcasting after giving up alcohol. The story was that he, too, had disappeared while on an assignment. Months later, a friend from Knoxville recognized him on a downtown Birmingham street, drunk, and managed to get him back to a relative in Tennessee.

Unlike Streetcar, he managed to stay sober, eventually establishing himself as a respected major-league sports broadcaster.

Such legends were repeated in late-night sessions around the copy desk, where the rim-rats and other late-shift veterans added credence to such tales by their own inebriated activity. The morgue, unoccupied after 5:30 p.m., offered plenty of hiding places for bottles in its filing cabinets. Or quick trips up the street to Lockett's were sometimes possible.

Too, there were the composing-room denizens who passed through the newsroom on their way to their jobs in the back shop. The saddest was a printer who maneuvered to the composing room by holding his hands out to touch each side of the long hallway as he carefully made his way to work. Years earlier he had, I was told, drunk an adulterated product known as "jake," which was produced during Prohibition and led to a kind of paralysis of the limbs.

The affliction was known as jakeleg, and that had become his nickname.

The contract that the printers' union had with The News-Sentinel Company (the Journal and the afternoon competition had a joint operating agreement, which meant that only the newsrooms were separate), specified that the printers could not drink alcohol on the job, but made no mention of "being drunk on the job." That was a distinction that was often brought up in set-to's involving the lead make-up man for the Journal.

As make-up editor for a couple of years, I spent about half my work shift in the composing room directing the printers as they put the pages together. I could not touch the type (union-contract rules), so I told the make-up men which story went where. This was in the days of hot type (fashioned from molten lead), and required that I be able to read copy upside down and backwards, skills that I picked up quickly because of necessity. Primarily, I worked with the lead make-up man, who put together Page One and the run-over page.

Most nights, the lead make-up man was a combative, diminutive veteran who was known to all by his nickname. I'll call him Blackie here. Most nights he was drunk. The shop steward (the union's on-site representative) operated a Linotype machine only a few feet away from the spot where Page One was worked. When the foreman accused Blackie of drinking on the job, the steward would point out that Blackie might be drunk, but it could not be proven that he was drinking on the job. Then, depending on how drunk he was, Blackie would sometimes challenge the foreman to a fight, and they would then glare at each other. This game was played once a month or so.

Often, when Blackie would disappear, a common occurrence, one of the other make-up men would cover for him by finishing his work on Page One. And once, when I had had a particularly trying experience with a particularly drunken Blackie, I turned to the shop steward and told him that I was going to finish the page, effectively daring him to order a union walkout. He glanced at me, then turned back to his Lintotype. I put the last two stories into the block. No one mentioned my transgression, and Blackie behaved himself for a few shifts.

Two long-time rim-rats had been banished to the copy desk because of their drinking and resultant un-reliability. One was excellent at his job, no matter his alcohol consumption. He lived in the mountains about 40 miles away from the office, and sometimes he would stay the night at my house instead of making the long drive home. When he did I would hear him making his way to our bar for a drink a couple of times during the night.

The other rim-rat drinker eventually followed in the footsteps of Streetcar, dismissed from the newspaper one last time, and several months later found dead on the street.

The wire editor, a daytime employee who had a wooden leg, would, a couple of times a year, get drunk while at work. These escapades happened, I was told by long-timers, only when his wife was out of town visiting her family.

Invariably his drinking would lead to a couple of days of missed work. The drunker he got, the more trouble he had with his prosthetic leg – he would begin to wobble. And that would lead to inflammation of his stump, which ended just above his knee. He would be unable to walk for a while.

One long-time sports writer was also known for periodic episodes involving drink. He would wander into the office after a bout with his friends and generally get in the way of those actually working.

One of the tales told about him had happened in the late 1950s, when he was scheduled to cover an upcoming Tennessee-Maryland football game that was being played in College Park. He somehow confused it with a later game against North Carolina and flew to Raleigh. Management finally got him back to Knoxville.

Another time, while I was working sports late one night, he came in looking for his teeth. He had somehow misplaced his false upper. After rummaging around his desk (always a mess), he left muttering about not understanding why anyone would want to steal his teeth.

Though the drinkers sometimes provided entertainment, their lives most often ended sadly. Eventually, that was what happened with Speedy. His final dismissal led a cohort and me to his apartment a couple of days later to check on him. He was there, and we surmised after noticing high heels and a stocking on the living-room floor, so was a girlfriend. He assured us that he would be okay.

After taking the cure (we referred to it as "going to whisky school"), he stayed sober for several years. After I had left Knoxville and would return periodically to visit, my sister, who knew one of Speedy's female friends, would give me reports. It was from her I learned that he had died, age 56.

~~~~~~~~~~

OF COURSE, ALCOHOL consumption was not the only vice practiced by the newsroom fixtures. As recreational drug use during the Sixties became more common, late-night shifts sometimes included marijuana breaks by the younger staffers.

A female reporter, an on-again, off-again UT student, established her credentials among the youngsters in the newsroom when she stole marijuana plants from the cops while covering the police beat.

A couple of officers who had confiscated several dozen mature plants called her, wanting publicity. They asked if they could stop by in their cruiser so the Journal photographer could get pictures of a trunkful of marijuana. She made the arrangements and met them outside the office. The photos were snapped, she got the information, and then managed to steal several of the plants by slipping them under the skirt of the "granny" dress she was wearing.

But the vibe of 1967's Summer of Love was long since over, and harder drugs had begun showing up on the streets around UT. An incident at a gathering centered on beer and marijuana at a friend's house sometime in 1969 was an eye-opener to several of us. One of the participants tied off and shot up heroin, eliciting a, "Have you no shame?" from the host.

My sole encounter with harder drugs involved LSD. A co-worker and I took a dose that he supplied one Friday evening. My memory of the episode is of playing "I Heard It Through the Grapevine" by Creedence Clearwater Revival on the stereo – over and over and over. Then, after a restless effort at trying to sleep, having flashbacks for the next day and a half. Interesting, I decided, but no more.

Besides the drinkers, the newsroom also had its share of philanderers. One in particular stood out. The Duffer, as I'll call him here, was married and had children. He was not shy about his conquests, and he was not picky about where his assignations took place.

The society department's office was a late-night favorite for a while. On at least one occasion, he rendezvoused with a prostitute at the quieter of the two downtown poolrooms, paying the manager to guard the front door while he and his partner made use of the snooker table at the back of the room.

The Duffer was a friend of Hazel Davidson, a notorious Knoxville prostitute and madam who was responsible for destroying the marriages of at least two prominent local businessmen.

Hazel would sometimes phone him at work to let him know about a new girl she was hosting – and also bring him up to date with what was happening at her establishment. If we were around, the Duffer would let Grady Amann and I know that Hazel was on the line, and we would pick up extensions and listen in. Hazel loved passing along stories of kinky clients, and her knowledge of Knoxville's underside was encyclopedic. That meant the Duffer's was, too.

During the early 1970s, downtown's Bijou specialized in showing X-rated movies, and one night Grady and I let the Duffer talk us into spending our dinner hour in the darkened theater.

He had an advantage over us in that he didn't have to return to work as quickly as we did. Contending that he wanted to see how the movie ended, the Duffer stayed when we got up to leave.

On the walk back, we hatched a plan. As soon as we were at our desks, Grady phoned the Bijou, telling whoever answered that there was an emergency at work and asking him to page the Duffer. As one of the lead writers covering UT sports, the Duffer was a popular Knoxville reporter. Shortly after our phone call, he was also known, at least to a dozen or so movie-goers, as a patron of the Bijou's X-rated fare.

Within a few minutes he was back in the office, not too happy with us.

But the Duffer generally tried to stay on good terms with me – I let him borrow my spare bedroom while I was at work. Eventually, a chance incident scared him into finding another place. The time was late afternoon, after the husband of the Duffer's paramour had gone to work. In bed, they were suddenly startled by someone pounding on the front door. The woman quickly hid in the closet, and the Duffer hunkered down in the bed. The pounding continued for a few minutes, then stopped, only to resume at the back door.

Finally, the noise ceased and, after determining that the source was gone, the Duffer and his friend got away from my house. When he got back to the office, he told me what had happened.

I had no idea as to the identity of the caller. But I found out the next day when Pat Fields, my landlady, told me that a county process server had caught up with her that morning – she owed back taxes on my house. I let the Duffer sweat, never informing him as to the reason for the door-knocking.

~~~~~~~~~~

IT WAS ABOUT this time that a Hollywood movie company came to town to make "The Lolly Madonna War," the story of a pair of feuding hillbilly clans.

The stars were Rod Steiger and Robert Ryan, and they and the crew were filming near Washburn in adjoining Union County.

Lolly Madonna was the name of the female character central to the movie's plot. And, thanks to my being employed by the Journal, she provided me with the opportunity to become a pornographer. An opportunity, I should add, that did not work out despite my best efforts.

Perhaps surprisingly, Knoxville didn't take much notice of the celebrity presence. I'm sure that had much to do with the set being on the far edge of civilization. Or maybe

Knoxvillians had become blasé to such Hollywood royalty –
we had, after all, hosted Anthony Quinn and Ingrid Bergman
only a couple of years earlier as they filmed a movie in
nearby Sevier County.

But Lolly Madonna's publicist was working to change that. Or
at least seemed to be as he took to hanging out at the Journal
office, mostly around a female reporter with whom he had
established a rapport.

The Journal published a handful of stories – but, as I recall,
the two veteran stars were savvy enough to avoid the
publicist and any media representatives trailing him.

So he came up with a plan to garner some national ink. He
was, he told those of us who would listen, buddies with
someone at Penthouse magazine, the then-upstart challenger
to Playboy. And that person, he was sure, would welcome a
photo feature involving a comely female wearing little or
nothing.

His plan was to find such a subject, make her an assistant
script girl, and then have a photographer take pictures on the
set that Penthouse would publish, providing pulchritudinous
publicity.

The Journal's veteran photographers, blessed with the clear-
eyed skepticism that experience brings, would have nothing
to do with his plan. So, at the suggestion of his female friend,
he approached me, a burgeoning photographer. And I, of
course, agreed to see if I could find a star-struck subject.

Several phone calls later, I realized that the girls I knew – UT students – were too smart for such a scheme. And none of them had any interest in meeting Rod Steiger or Robert Ryan – after I had explained to them who they were. I realized that most children of the Sixties had little knowledge of stars from the days of black and white films.

And I had to admit that what interest I had in yet another project exploiting the stereotypical ignorant hillbilly was quickly waning. I did attempt one trip to the location site but got lost. My efforts to get help finding my way back to Knoxville did provide an example of Appalachian isolation.

In Washburn, I stopped in a country grocery seeking directions. The teen-aged girl behind the counter – I would guess her age at 16 or 17 – said she didn't know and confessed to never having been to Knoxville, all of 30 miles away.

So I didn't get around to visiting the movie set and soon forgot about the movie, which garnered little attention when it was released.

But occasionally Turner Classic Movies airs "Lolly Madonna XXX" – the title had been changed, with the Xs meant to represent kisses. Unfortunately, the triple Xs gave the impression that the movie was pornographic. Maybe the publicist from the early 1970s had suggested the name change.

So, I watched it 40 years after its release. And discovered that it is certainly worth a couple of hours of time, the two stars and their fellow actors delivering excellent performances following a credible and well-written script.

The supporting cast, a mixture of veteran Hollywood character actors and newcomers, included three boys who went on to make big-screen names for themselves, names that would have been recognizable to any girls I might have contacted if I was seeking an assistant script girl a generation or so later: Jeff Bridges, Gary Busey and Randy Quaid.

And Lolly Madonna? She existed in name only – the "sender" of a prank postcard that set off a murderous rampage.

~~~~~~~~~~

UNION COUNTY was an appropriate site for a movie involving violent escapades that end in murder. Around the newsroom, we referred to it as "beyond civilization," a reference I was reminded of a couple of years later when I made a return visit after I had moved to Miami. A friend asked if I wanted to go to a cockfight – in Union County.

A biology master's student, he was working part-time at Oak Ridge Associated Universities in a program involving cancer research. A couple of his co-workers had invited him along.

So the four of us set out one Saturday night for the fight site, deep in the Union County backwoods. The facility was a large, round barn, and the surrounding field was crowded with trucks and cars when we arrived.

After paying the $2 entry fee, we picked up a card with The Bull Run Game Club's schedule, which listed eight months of meetings, every-other week. Some events were "cock," others "stag", a couple included a "short heel" designation.

At the bottom of the card, in bold-face type, was a warning: NO DRINKING ALLOWED.

This was to be my first and only visit to a cockfight, but my introduction to the culture had occurred several years earlier, courtesy of the father of one of my sister's acquaintances. In his east Knoxville backyard, he had shown me a couple of roosters that he was conditioning. He told me that he didn't fight them but was helping a friend who did.

The subject was interesting enough that I wrote down what he had told me when I returned home, figuring that I might want to write about the subject at some point.

My decades-old notes, refreshed by internet searches, reveal that a stag is a bird less than 2 years old, a cock older than 2. A short heel is a steel "knife" about an inch long that is attached to the bird's foot to replace its natural spur, which has been cut off.

My source had made me a gift of a pair of spurs that he had recently trimmed off in order to substitute needle-like steel "gaffs," more deadly than the knives. And he pointed out the rooster's hackles, the feathers on the back of its neck. When the hackles are up, he said, the bird is anxious to fight.

My notes and my spurs had been filed away when I left Knoxville in 1972.

When my companions and I entered the Union County barn, we found a raucous crowd sitting on benches, about six rows ascending around a circular pit. The birds, small bundles of feathers in high states of excitement, reminded me of what my grandmother called "banty roosters." Two men, holding their birds, were perched on the concrete-block wall that defined the pit, preparing to turn the roosters loose.

As we looked around, we realized that despite the admonition against alcohol, many of the attendees had obviously been drinking. There were numerous trips outside to vehicles parked in the field surrounding the barn. No drinking inside maybe, but what you did out in the field or in your truck was your own business. And, after a refreshment break, re-entry to the barn was not a problem.

The birds were matched by weight, and their owners carried them around the edge of the ring, letting the bettors take them in.

Bets were yelled out: "Ten on the Blue;" "I got 50 on the Roundhead;" "Who wants 20 against the Hackel?" A couple of men were circling just outside the pit, noting the wagers, making sure that the bettors knew who had responded to their calls.

Bets laid, the first match began with the two roosters rushing at each other. Feathers and blood were soon flying. Breaks would include the handlers wiping blood away and breathing into the cocks' mouths.

After a while, one of the birds was unable to continue, and a victor was declared. Money changed hands around the barn, and the next match began. Soon, the "drag pit" behind the bleachers was occupied with barely alive birds that could continue only sporadically. Once they had expired, the dead were carried outside. I didn't inquire as to their disposal.

After a couple of hours, we decided we had seen enough and departed. Later, my friend said his co-workers were getting up another trip to the game club's meeting. Did I want to go?

I declined and he admitted he had no interest either.

He had decided that his acquaintances were a bit odd and didn't want to hang out with them anymore. "They're dieners," he said. What's that? I asked.

"They help out at autopsies," he explained.

~~~~~~~~~~

LONG BEFORE I left Knoxville in 1972, my partying days had wound down, a result of what I was seeing around me: the old hands on the copy desk, the tales involving Blackie and Streetcar and other legendary Journal drinkers, watching the deterioration of Speedy.

At about the same time, I knew I wanted to leave the Journal, to leave Knoxville. More and more, my reading involved national magazines such as Esquire, The Atlantic, The New Yorker, where the stories were longer and more comprehensive. And my viewpoint, always liberal, had become more skeptical – I was following the work of Paul Krassner in The Realist and Cavalier. Scanlon's Review, a leading muckraking periodical of the time, was also on my must-read list.

The final push came from an unexpected quarter. Thanks to late-night grousing around the copy desk, to general unhappiness about the way work was going, a handful of us decided that we should unionize the newsroom. And I decided that my contribution to such an effort would be an appropriate farewell to the Journal.

The News-Sentinel operation was already union, from the reporters to the pressmen. The Journal newsroom was the only operation in the building that was not. So, when we decided to organize and force a vote for representation by The Newspaper Guild, we could count on the support of the other unions in the building. Maybe, we joked, the pressmen would even start a fire in the Press Room for us.

So we contacted Guild headquarters in Washington, D.C., and they sent a representative to meet with us. A Knoxville attorney, the late Robert Ritchie, was hired to assist us, and the Journal publisher was notified of our intentions.

The Journal brought in an Atlanta law firm that specialized in anti-union work. One of the attorneys they sent to Knoxville was a UT graduate I had known when I was a student. He and I would sometimes trade good-natured barbs when our paths crossed.

The effort took about a year and ended several newsroom friendships, as we ostracized those who refused to join us. Since I was the late-night news editor, an effort was made to exclude me from the voting unit. The effort failed because, in a classic Journal move, I did not receive a raise in pay when I assumed those duties.

When I was questioned (under oath) before the judge from the National Labor Relations Board, I exasperated my old friend from UT days by making him repeat every question. My cohorts who followed me used the same tactic.

We won the election by a slim margin. And, having already settled my financial affairs (such as they were), I purchased an airline ticket for Luxembourg. In mid-August, armed with a Eurail Pass and enough high-school French to get myself into trouble, I caught a train for Brussels, where I was to meet with Al Webb, the head of United Press International's European operations and another alumnus of the Journal.

Unfortunately for my co-workers, Journal management, using their political clout, managed to get the union decision moved into federal court where the results were thrown out. A new vote was ordered and the Guild lost. By then, I was somewhere in the Austrian Alps, having swapped my native ridges for much taller mountains in a completely different world.

--30--

Acknowledgements

This memoir of growing up in Knoxville could not have happened without the help of many of those who experienced it with me. Some are identified in the stories with which they are associated; the names of most story participants have been changed.

Those who contributed memories of escapades that sparked my own recollections included childhood neighbors Danny Meador, Joyce Maskall Wishart, Anita McGuire Melia and the late Vincent Kanipe and Vance Walker. Others who provided details include fellow members of Boy Scout Troop 15, classmates at Park Junior High School and East High School, and my late siblings, sister Johanna and brother Ben.

Compatriots at The Knoxville Journal, especially Grady Amann and the late Ben Byrd, provided stories where they were participants as well as details of adventures we all witnessed.

Characters from places I frequented in the late 1960s and early 1970s created vivid memories of hours wasted – at the Yardarm and Brownie's in the University of Tennessee area, Opal's Tap Room in south Knoxville, Blaufeld's lunch counter and McDonald's pool hall downtown, Bill's Barn (open 24 hours) in Bearden and others.

The tumultuous five years I spent at UT provided rich fodder. Helping bring the memories into focus were Tom Jester, Jim Bennett, Rusty Brashear, Steve Horne, John Pittman, Bob

Selwyn, Danny West, Cathy Jones, Vince Staten and the late Tom Stokes.

Cousins Bob and Tim Guinn and Judy and Cindy Wohlwend contributed family recollections.

Coury Turczyn and Matthew Everett of The Knoxville Mercury newspaper generously agreed to publish my column, "Restless Native," and most of those stories became elements of this memoir. The Sixties history of the UT pop-music scene also was published in the Mercury, in slightly different form.

Early in this project, Keith Graham and Lee Leslie of Like the Dew website indulged me by posting several stories that became "Ridge Running" components. The profile of mountain man JR Buchanan originally appeared in The Atlanta Journal-Constitution.

Publication could not have happened without the computer expertise of John McNair, Anne Hensley, Clint Elmore, and publisher Jim Stovall of First Inning Press. Dennis and Judy McCarthy generously read the manuscript and offered insight. Lisa Byerley Gary's sharp-eyed proofreading guaranteed coherence. And Doug Monroe provided editing expertise, wise advice, and encouragement.

Made in the USA
Lexington, KY
30 July 2019